TRAVIS COLLINS

WHAT DOES IT MEAN TO BE WELCOMING

?

NAVIGATING LGBT QUESTIONS IN YOUR CHURCH

IVP Books

An imprint of InterVarsity Press
Downers Grove, Illinois

InterVarsity Press
P.O. Box 1400, Downers Grove, IL 60515-1426
ivpress.com
email@ivpress.com

InterVarsity Press® is the book-publishing division of InterVarsity Christian Fellowship/USA®, a movement of students and faculty active on campus at hundreds of universities, colleges, and schools of nursing in the United States of America, and a member movement of the International Fellowship of Evangelical Students. For information about local and regional activities, visit intervarsity.org.

All Scripture quotations, unless otherwise indicated, are taken from The Holy Bible, New International Version®, NIV®. Copyright © 1973, 1978, 1984, 2011 by Biblica, Inc.™ Used by permission of Zondervan. All rights reserved worldwide. www.zondervan.com. The "NIV" and "New International Version" are trademarks registered in the United States Patent and Trademark Office by Biblica, Inc.™

While any stories in this book are true, some names and identifying information may have been changed to protect the privacy of individuals.

Content from "A Krispy Kreme for the Road" sermon in chapter two used by permission of Bon Air Baptist Church, Richmond, Virginia.

Cover design: David Fassett
Interior design: Daniel van Loon
Images: colored flag: © skdesigns / Digital Vision Vectors / Getty Images

ISBN 978-0-8308-4144-8 (print)
ISBN 978-0-8308-7418-7 (digital)

Printed in the United States of America ∞

Library of Congress Cataloging-in-Publication Data
Names: Collins, Travis, author.
Title: What does it mean to be welcoming? : navigating LGBT questions in your
   church / Travis Collins.
Description: Downers Grove : InterVarsity Press, 2018. | Includes
   bibliographical references.
Identifiers: LCCN 2018014460 (print) | LCCN 2018022328 (ebook) | ISBN
   9780830874187 (eBook) | ISBN 9780830841448 (pbk. : alk. paper)
Subjects: LCSH: Sexual minorities—Religious life. | Sex role—Religious
   aspects—Christianity.
Classification: LCC BV4596.G38 (ebook) | LCC BV4596.G38 C655 2018 (print) |
   DDC 261.8/35766—dc23
LC record available at https://lccn.loc.gov/2018014460

P   25 24 23 22 21 20 19 18 17 16 15 14 13 12 11 10 9 8 7 6 5 4 3 2 1

Y   37 36 35 34 33 32 31 30 29 28 27 26 25 24 23 22 21 20 19 18

"At a time when many churches find themselves unprepared and ill-equipped to engage the questions of human sexuality that define our culture, this book is a most welcome resource! Written by a pastor for pastors, *What Does It Mean to Be Welcoming?* is a compelling guide for church leaders who are committed to navigating LGBT conversations in their communities with the sort of honesty and humility that ought to mark all Christian discourse. Unthoughtful, fear driven polarization will likely continue over these issues, but Collins offers a richer vision of faithful Christian witness that we desperately need in our churches."

JR Rozko, codirector at Missio Alliance

"In the plethora of positions and the maze of materials on this topic, Travis Collins's book is a welcome summary from a thinking pastor's heart. *What Does It Mean to Be Welcoming?* demonstrates clarity, sensitivity, and the desire to guard the unity of the body as we struggle honestly together to apply the gospel of grace and truth. It has been a breath of fresh air in the midst of what is often a polarizing issue fraught with vitriol and hostility."

Bill White, senior pastor of Christ Journey Church in Coral Gables, Florida

"In *What Does It Mean to Be Welcoming?* Travis Collins offers not a diatribe, but a conversation. Pastoral in tone, careful in scholarship, he guides us through the maze that is the current divide over same-sex sexual relations in the church. We may differ in approach, but I greatly appreciate this clarifying work."

David Fitch, B. R. Lindner Chair of Evangelical Theology at Northern Seminary, author of *Faithful Presence*

"Travis Collins has done a masterful job of providing a practical and pastoral application to the most challenging issue facing the church today. *What Does It Mean to Be Welcoming?* is an essential resource for churches that seek to be proactive, gracious, and redemptive in their approach to the many questions surrounding LGBT topics."

Phillip Faig, senior pastor, Downtown Baptist Church, Alexandria, Virginia

"It's not just *what* Travis Collins wrote or *why* he wrote it that makes this a valuable book. It's also *how* he wrote it. In *What Does It Mean to Be Welcoming?* you'll find the complex topic of sexuality and the church unpacked with a central view of Christ and a purposeful, compassionate view of humanity. As a friend of Travis, I am not surprised by this. He writes what he lives and he lives what he writes—with evident conviction, wisdom, thoughtfulness, patience, and humility."

J. R. Briggs, founder of Kairos Partnerships, author of *Fail: Finding Hope and Grace in the Midst of Ministry Failure*

"If you are in search of a thoughtful, accessible, pastoral guide to help your congregation or even denomination conduct the fraught conversation regarding same-sex relationships, then allow me to commend to you this valuable volume by my friend and ministerial colleague Dr. Travis Collins. Whether you embrace or are inclined to hold an affirming or a traditionalist view, there is much to learn from and ponder over in *What Does It Mean to Be Welcoming?*, which can in turn inform personal and ecclesial practice. In a day when more heat than light surrounds this complex, controverted matter, such a resource is both timely and necessary."

Todd D. Still, Charles J. and Eleanor McLerran DeLancey Dean and William M. Hinson Professor of Christian Scriptures at Baylor University

TO THE PEOPLE

OF FIRST BAPTIST CHURCH,

HUNTSVILLE, ALABAMA,

WHO LOVE AND SUPPORT ME

FAR BEYOND WHAT I DESERVE.

CONTENTS

"WELCOMING?"

AN INTRODUCTION

"ALL ARE WELCOME HERE, as we are, as we are."

In the contemporary worship service at the church I serve, we frequently sing those words from Eddie Kirkland's song "Here and Now."[1] Every time we sing them, I wonder what people are thinking: *Do people really believe that? Do people believe us when we say, "All are welcome"?*

So I wasn't surprised when our contemporary worship leader recently told me that every time we sing "All are welcome here, as we are," someone asks him afterward, "Is that really true?"

Do all people actually feel welcome in our place? After all, as a congregation we did issue a Traditionalist statement on sexuality. That statement does not, in any way, exclude people from worship, fellowship, or membership in our church based on sexual orientation or behavior. And it certainly does not state that anyone is unwelcome here. But because of our decision, some (regretfully) don't feel welcomed.

So what does "welcoming" mean—really? That is what we are talking about in this book.

When church leaders wrestle with LGBT questions, we are not talking about whether same-sex attracted people are to be respected, or whether they should be allowed to live wherever they want, or whether they should be able to visit their partners in critical care units of hospitals, or whether their families should love and embrace them. Those are easy questions, and the obvious answer to all of them (for me, at least) is an enthusiastic *Yes*.

We are considering much more difficult questions. We are talking about what it means for a church to say they are "welcoming."

We're talking about whether that wonderful woman who is at church every Sunday, who brings snacks every week to youth night, and who we know is in a same-sex relationship should be asked to teach the senior high school girls Sunday school class next year.

We are talking about what the minister should do when the chairman of the church board asks that minister to perform the wedding ceremony for the chairman's lesbian daughter and her partner.

We are talking about what we should tell the teens in our student ministries about same-sex intimacy, or if we should say anything at all.

We are talking about whether your church or denomination should ordain that young man who grew up in your church, is the best young preacher you've ever heard, and is in a same-sex relationship.

We're talking about whether you should leave your church, or whether your church should leave your denomination, over this. We might even be talking about whether your church might get kicked out of your denominational family over this.

We're also talking about whether these are even going to be questions twenty years from now.

I probably should acknowledge that there are lots of topics and arguments, such as the mushrooming transgender debate, about which my lack of expertise prevents me from adding anything helpful. So, admittedly, there are important LGBT concerns that will go unaddressed in this book. My focus will be on same-sex relationships.

One of the most difficult decisions in writing this book was the choice of language. Because my focus here will be on lesbian, gay, and bisexual relationships, I will primarily use the words *same-sex attracted*, *same-sex relationships*, and *same-sex intimacy*. When I use the term *gay*, I'm using it as a synonym for *same-sex attracted* even though I know not everyone considers these words synonyms. In addition, I discuss *attraction*, *orientation*, and *identity* in chapter seven.

It is difficult to find terms to refer to the two sides of this conversation. Any term I considered could be interpreted as biased, disparaging, or inaccurate. I finally settled on Affirming and Traditionalist. Generally speaking, those on the Affirming side of the conversation believe we should allow for same-sex relationships, including marriage. On the other hand, Traditionalists advocate for a "traditional" interpretation of Scripture and are not affirming of same-sex relationships, including marriage. I use these terms with no prejudice toward either, and ask that you understand my intent behind their use. I plead for understanding from those who, from whatever perspective, might find my choices of language frustrating.

In this book you will come across words such as *topic*, *subject*, and *matter*. Same-sex relationships are indeed a hot topic, a complicated subject, and an important matter.

This conversation, however, is not about dispassionate topics, academic subjects, and isolated matters. This is a conversation about people—people created in the image of God. People who love and are loved. People whose lives are affected by our words. If I appear overly theoretical on any of these pages then I will not have communicated my emotional investment in this conversation.

This has been a very personal journey over a number of years. I have found myself at odds with close friends. I have felt the hurt of Christians who have been maligned, and I have been maligned personally. I have experienced just about every emotion imaginable along the way. I have been angered, affirmed, offended, emboldened, conflicted, confused, encouraged, and afraid. I stand where I stand firmly, but I stand here humbly and compassionately—with a few arrows in my hide from both sides of this emotional debate.

My heart, in the broadest and deepest sense, is in this.

I write this as the pastor of a big tent church that recently wrestled with, and issued a position statement on, the topic of human sexuality. I write this as a close friend of many church leaders whose churches and denominations are in tough conversations surrounding sexuality. I've been living with this topic for a long time, and if this book is of help to church leaders, it would be my honor.

So, how might you use this book? (Well, you're obviously reading it, so that's one way to use it!) Beyond that, however, I have a number of particular uses in mind.

CHURCHES

Of course I write this as a pastor, and I hope this will be of help to those who share my vocational calling. I understand how difficult this conversation is for congregational shepherds.

Yet I write this with laypersons in mind. Laypersons are usually interested in where the proverbial water hits the wheel. Laypersons are particularly practical, and encouragingly so, when it comes to discussions like this. People who make up the congregations I have served want to know both the whys and the hows. Therefore, I have provided here those things that devoted followers of Jesus are looking for, from biblical background to everyday implications. I even threw in a few stories to illustrate the "everyday-ness" of LGBT questions.

In the churches where I worked on this topic, we made copies of an earlier form of this book available church-wide (see Appendix A for a suggested process, including how you might use this book at your church). It helped to have people reading the same thing, using the same language. The length and scope of this book were planned with that use in mind. I believe it will be helpful to make copies of the book available to all those people who are interested and to those who will be making decisions about the course your church will take.

SMALL GROUPS AND SUNDAY SCHOOL CLASSES

This book provides a brief but thorough study of a topic on the minds and hearts of lots of people. You can have a safe conversation within a circle of people who love and trust one another, and this book will facilitate that. The tone of this book lends itself to having people from differing perspectives read and discuss it.

DENOMINATIONS

LGBT questions dominate many denominational discussions nowadays. The widespread distribution of this book to pastors, church leaders, and denominational workers can work in the same way that the distribution of the book works among church members. It provides common language to use and common topics to consider. Even though I contend for a certain position, I represent opposing viewpoints so that even those who disagree with me are included in the discussion.

DISCUSSION QUESTIONS
Toward the end of this book you will find a discussion guide with questions for each part of the book. I hope these will be useful to you and your group as together we attempt to discern the mind of God, understand Holy Scripture, and love people.

PART ONE

THE
COMPLEXITY

CHAPTER ONE

MEANINGS, MOTIVES, REGRETS, AND HOPES

SINCE 1981 I HAVE BEEN either a missionary (seven of those years) or a pastor (the rest of those years). I've seen churches split over the charismatic movement. I've seen a great deal of mud slung over women in ministry. I've seen Calvinists and Arminians square off. Yet never have I witnessed the pain, demonization, and honest soul-searching that I've seen surrounding the church's response to LGBT questions.

Our reputations and relationships are at risk. Same-sex attracted people are vulnerable in so many ways. The hearts of people who deeply love same-sex attracted persons are laid bare. Some see this as a battle for the soul of the church. The stakes are so high it's sobering.

Given that, let's begin here: there will be significant disagreements on this subject among people who love your church, love the Bible, and love Jesus. We absolutely must be respectful of one another in our discussions.

Across the country, in congregations like yours and almost certainly including yours, there are people who have same-sex attraction. Others are learning how to respond to news from family members about those family members' gay identities. This is a tender matter for many, and every time we talk about this we should assume we are in the presence of someone who either is same-sex attracted or loves someone who is.

I will not deny my personal trepidation as I write. To begin with, I prefer to have people like and admire me. What I say about this topic sometimes makes a difference in the way people view me and my leadership, so I admit my consternation.

More importantly, I have a knot in my stomach because I don't want to cause harm. I don't want to hurt or alienate the gay and lesbian community. I don't want to ignite the flames of division in anyone's church. I don't want to imply even a trace of disparagement toward those who will disagree with my position.

For whatever it's worth, then, please know the weight I feel in writing this book. If it were not such an important topic, I would gladly have avoided it.

I believe my primary job in writing this is to do my best to be someone who "correctly handles the word of truth" (2 Timothy 2:15). I believe your primary job is to decide if what I'm saying is true to Scripture (Acts 17:11). Neither one of us can abdicate our roles.

You deserve to know my stance up front. I will state it rather simplistically here, and then plead with you to read this entire book and let me unpack these words. The phrase that best describes my position is "Welcoming but Not Affirming and Mutually Transforming." "Welcoming but Not Affirming" is a phrase made popular by Stanley Grenz. "Welcoming and Mutually Transforming" was coined by David Fitch. We will look at both phrases in this book.

In short, Welcoming but Not Affirming and Mutually Transforming means that (1) I welcome all people to membership in the church family; (2) I do not affirm same-sex sexual behavior; and (3) I believe all of us are called to be transformed into the image of Jesus, and we all are still in process. I hope you will continue reading to see what all that means. With those preliminaries, let me offer some personal reflections.

PEOPLE ON BOTH SIDES ARE DRIVEN BY ADMIRABLE MOTIVES

While both sides have their narrow-minded, acrimonious crusaders, this debate is usually between people with good hearts. Faithful followers of Jesus who hold progressive views on same-sex matters are motivated by compassion and an admirable desire for fairness (often referred to as justice). They are compelled by a passion for equal and nondiscriminatory treatment of everyone. I know stories of people whose watershed moments came while facing the awful reality of racial discrimination and who want to be sure we do not make the sinful mistake of discriminating against same-sex attracted people.

The views of many who support same-sex relationships grow out of the belief that it simply could not be God's will that someone have a same-sex attraction (through no choice of their own) and not be able to live a fulfilling life with a devoted companion. Furthermore, every Affirming person I know admirably believes a church has a spiritual imperative to reach out to those on the margins, whether they are on the margins because of race, economics, social standing, or any other reason, including sexual attraction. My friends who I disagree with on the same-sex topic are kindhearted, generous Christians who simply want what is best for others. I cringe when I hear them mischaracterized.

There are those whose Affirming positions have been costly. People have lost jobs and friendships because they have courageously stated their convictions. I have pastor friends whose character has been maligned and whose churches have lost members because of the pastors' willingness to go public with their affirmation of same-sex marriage. I admire their courage and integrity, even though I disagree with their position.

Likewise, Traditionalists—those who affirm sexual intimacy only between a married man and woman—demonstrate admirable motives. People I know who hold a Traditional position on marriage and sexuality are not driven by hatred or fear (despite common charges to the contrary) but by their love for God, which compels them to hold to the authority of Scripture. They are trying to follow the example of Jesus and live out both grace and truth. Candidly, it angers me that so many on the Affirming side attempt to claim the exclusive high ground on love and justice. That is, I believe, a weak and indefensible mischaracterization of people on the Traditional side of this debate.

LABELS AREN'T HELPING

One of the disappointing things surrounding this debate within the Christian family is the labeling of our spiritual siblings. On the one hand, some Traditionalists accuse those on the Affirming side of not caring anything about the Bible, and sometimes even challenge the sincerity of their Christian faith. Those who do not affirm same-sex intimacy can be terribly harsh in their assessment of those who see the matter differently.

Yet those who advocate same-sex intimacy within committed relationships can be equally ruthless, often accusing those on the other side of being haters, afraid, and intolerant. Narrow-mindedness and intolerance are not limited to those on the right; there is also a fundamentalism from the left that is poisoning our culture. Labeling people we disagree with squashes healthy dialogue and makes us all look bad.

THIS ISN'T JUST A GENERATIONAL THING

It's true that surveys demonstrate generational differences on lots of topics, including gay orientation and behavior. But to suggest that different convictions regarding LGBT topics are primarily generational is arrogant, lazy, and an insult to all generations!

It makes younger generations seem naïve, impulsive, immature, and not yet capable of a well-thought-out decision. It makes older generations seem obstinate, dense, and unable to change their minds even if confronted with new information. It is more helpful to set aside age differences and have a kind but candid conversation about biblical evidence and interpretation.

TRADITIONALISTS SHOULD CHANGE SOME ASSUMPTIONS

Of course, I regret the assumptions many people make about those who do not affirm same-sex intimacy ("They are bigots, homophobes, and Neanderthals"). Yet, as one who holds a Traditional view of marriage and sexuality, I want to acknowledge the unfortunate assumptions about gay people made by many who share my position. Stereotypes have not been helpful in our consideration of LGBT topics, so let me try and correct a few.

- Same-sex attracted people are not all on a crusade to force their opinions on to everyone else. There are those who simply want to live their lives without changing mine. It is wrong to assume every gay person is a militant activist.

- The relationships of gay couples are not, as some would claim, inevitably unhappy. I know gay people in monogamous, long-lasting, committed relationships who appear to be as happy as many straight couples I know.

- It is wrong to assume that children of gay couples are more maladjusted than those of straight couples. I do believe a mother and a father together provide the best potential for an ideal home, and I do believe that is God's design. But I know sons and daughters of gay couples who are well-adjusted people.

- All gay people don't hate or even resent people like me who have a Traditional view of marriage and sexuality. They don't all think that I, and people like me who share a Traditional view of sexuality, are bigots, homophobes, and Neanderthals.

LET'S MOVE PAST ARGUMENTS OVER THE "CAUSE" OF SAME-SEX ATTRACTION

A debate still rages over the reasons behind same-sex attraction. And whether or not one believes the root of same-sex attraction is nature or nurture often depends on which side of the debate one is on.

Affirmers often point to what they say are innate physiological reasons, such as hormonal or genetic influences, behind same-sex attraction. They contend that God created some people as same-sex attracted and if that is how God made them, we should bless same-sex relationships. Surely, Affirmers contend, we don't expect people who are made gay by God to miss out on the joys of intimacy.

Many Traditionalists argue that same-sex attraction is not inborn. They contend that it is a matter of arrested sexual development, some irregularity in one's upbringing, or pure choice. After all, if God "made them this way" it would be necessary to explain how God would then not expect gay persons to live out their God-given sexual orientation.

The evidence actually points to a confluence of factors. Same-sex attraction almost certainly results from a combination of nature and nurture, some convergence of genetics and environment. Certainly, the evidence points to strong, innate factors. What seems absolutely clear is that the attraction is not the choice of the person. The behavior is a choice, but not the attraction.

Frankly, we don't know all the reasons why someone is same-sex attracted. And it would solve nothing if we *could* know.

To me, it seems most prudent to acknowledge our ignorance regarding *why* someone is same-sex attracted and focus on what people do with that same-sex attraction. As a Traditionalist, I won't be in the least surprised or deterred if, one day, some irrefutable proof is offered that the neurology and biology of straight people are somehow and slightly different from that of gay people. I still will want to include gay people in the circle and also encourage their abstinence (more on that later).

Remember the story from John 9 of the man born blind:

> His [Jesus'] disciples asked him, "Rabbi, who sinned, this man or his parents, that he was born blind?"
>
> "Neither this man nor his parents sinned," said Jesus, "but this happened so that the works of God might be displayed in him." (John 9:2-3)

I believe we cannot speak definitively to the origin of same-sex attraction. We can, however, live a life in which the powerful and grace-filled work of God is displayed and lovingly encourage others to do the same.

LET'S MOVE BEYOND PLACING BLAME
ON PARENTAL "MISSTEPS"

It is misguided to assign "blame" to the parents of people who are gay. There are almost certainly a myriad of factors contributing to an attraction to those of one's own sex. To make the assumption that same-sex attraction is the disgraceful result of parental mistakes does not contribute anything helpful to the discussion. Such a crude supposition inevitably causes countless good parents to feel undeserved shame.

Author Justin Lee, a Christian man who is gay, says:

> I don't believe there's anything parents can do to prevent their children from being gay. I had strong, warm relationships with both of my parents, felt fully and completely loved, was given healthy amounts of discipline and independence, and everything else I've heard recommended to parents. If I turned out gay, any kid can turn out gay. Meanwhile, my three siblings turned out straight, and we all were raised by the same parents.
>
> Having a gay child doesn't necessarily mean parents did anything "wrong." Instead of blaming themselves, parents should focus on showing their child all the love they can and keeping their relationship strong as the family works together through the moral and theological questions they face.[1]

LET'S NOT SEND THE MESSAGE THAT WE'LL
LOVE PEOPLE ONLY IF THEY CHANGE

The subtle (and often not-so-subtle) message that some churches have sent to same-sex attracted people is that we will love and accept you if you will get treatment and become opposite-sex attracted. In the end, the insistence on a new sexual orientation has (1) proven to be an overly simplistic expectation and (2) been deeply hurtful for many Christians who cannot, despite their most prayerful and persistent efforts, "become heterosexual," yet wish to be faithful members of the church family.

Exodus International was a high-profile Christian ministry that for many years had the mission of championing and facilitating the "conversion" of same-sex attracted persons to heterosexuality. In 2013, however, Exodus closed up shop and acknowledged they had overpromised on the possibility of such re-orientation. Their message in closing was this: sexual re-orientation is possible, but not nearly as likely as many had believed.

Communicating to people with same-sex attraction that if they change and become straight *then* we'll accept them is simply sending the wrong message. Please understand: I don't want to imply limits on God's power to liberate us from anything that is less than God's best for us. I simply don't want to make our love for those who are same-sex attracted conditional on that liberation.

1 Corinthians 6:9-11 says:

> Do not be deceived: Neither the sexually immoral nor idolaters nor adulterers nor men who have sex with men nor thieves nor the greedy nor drunkards nor slanderers nor swindlers will inherit the kingdom of God. And that is what some of you were. But you were washed, you were sanctified, you were justified in the name of the Lord Jesus Christ and by the Spirit of our God.

That text makes all of us grateful for grace and hopeful for transformation. Yet I contend it is pushing the meaning of the text too far to suggest it guarantees sexual re-orientation if we will only believe deeply enough and work hard enough.

Author Rosaria Champagne Butterfield wrote this about her experience of converting to Christianity: "The God of the universe burst into my secular world and atheistic worldview in the person of Jesus Christ in 1999, when I was thirty-six years old, happily partnered in a lesbian relationship."[2] A dramatic sexual re-orientation such as Butterfield's confirms God's transformational power, but should not, I believe, be expected or demanded of every follower of Jesus.

"TOLERANCE" HAS BEEN REDEFINED

This is the age of a new kind of tolerance. The tolerance of yesterday meant we respected other people even though we disagreed with their positions. Today's tolerance means we must acknowledge all opinions and beliefs as equally valid. To talk of ultimate truth is to be charged with bigotry, fanaticism, fundamentalism, and closed-mindedness. Any sense of right and wrong thus disappears into a fog of "feel-good-ness."

It's one thing to confess, "I know I am greedy; please pray that I will become more others-centered." It's quite another to demand, "Please affirm my greediness!" My demand that you affirm something that is wrong in my life is a sentimentalized and untenable redefinition of tolerance.

We have moved rather quickly from "yes, same-sex intimacy is a sin, but so are lots of other things, such as pride and being judgmental" to "same-sex intimacy is not a sin." The former statement ("same-sex intimacy is a sin, but there are lots of others") is something every Traditionalist I know would agree is a given. The latter ("same-sex intimacy is not a sin at all"), however, is a leap Traditionalists cannot make.

To use the label of intolerant for a Traditionalist in this case is so obviously unfair it is disappointing that I have to mention it.

I KNOW THIS IS PERSONAL

Controversies are common in the Christian family. Did God create the universe in seven twenty-four-hour periods, or did he create it by means of evolution? Were Adam and Eve literal persons? Is the Bible God's revelation or *witness to* God's revelation? Should we say "inerrant," "infallible," or "inspired"? Was Calvin or Arminias right?

Debates over such matters can get heated . . . but they aren't personal. Eve (of Eden fame) is not someone's lesbian daughter. John Calvin is not someone's gay friend. When we debate theories of inspiration, there aren't names and stories attached— at least not in the same way that names and stories are attached to the topic here.

This conversation is personal. It is about people we know and love.

AND I KNOW THIS IS RISKY

I deeply appreciate the contribution of academics who have the expertise and courage to offer their insights to the larger Christian community. I am a grateful beneficiary of those insights. I know that many who minister in the world of academia take professional risks when they take positions on a topic as hotly debated as this.

When an accountable member of a church family takes a position, however, the risk is not only professional; the risk is also up close and personal. I have the highest respect for denominational and local church leaders who have so much riding on these difficult conversations. I know many of you are concerned for individuals affected by these conversations, for the congregations and denominations you serve, and perhaps even for your vocational future.

This is risky.

It is to the risky reality of divergent opinions within the same communities of faith that we now turn our attention.

CHAPTER TWO

A DIFFICULT, KNOTTY, POTENTIALLY THORNY CONVERSATION

THERE IS A REASON LGBT questions are dividing so many families and congregations. They're difficult. They're knotty. They can be thorny.

Everyone doesn't seem to understand the intricacies. I hear people on both sides of this argument make sincere but simplistic statements. On the one side, people declare, "The Bible is clear! Men having sex with men and women having sex with women is wrong. This is not hard to understand!" From the other side I hear, "The Bible says love God and love each other! We should just preach love and live love and not get caught up in other stuff." It's more complicated than either of those perspectives would indicate.

Certainly, the Bible's position on this seems clear to me. Yet the many intricacies, nuances, emotions, and conflicts make this a multi-faceted, multi-layered, and complicated discussion.

- It's complicated because good and intelligent people view this matter very differently.
- It's complicated because finding the balance between grace and truth is difficult—so difficult the pendulum often swings hard in one direction or the other.
- It's complicated because we are not talking about formulas or machines; we are talking about same-sex attracted

people—people created in God's image, people who love and are loved—not just theories and position statements.

Below are a few of the other complications.

WHERE SHOULD WE DRAW THE LINE?

This is a complicated question. In his book *A Letter to My Congregation*, Pastor Ken Wilson examines these words from an old hymn by Frederick Faber:

> But we make His love too narrow
> By false limits of our own;
>
> And we magnify His strictness
> With a zeal He will not own.[1]

Wilson is right to ask whether we are making God's "love too narrow by false limits of our own" and whether perhaps "we magnify His strictness with a zeal He will not own." If we are being more rigorous than God would be in the application of the biblical texts that address same-sex intimacy, and if by doing so we are excluding people from church leadership and meaningful relationships that God himself would include, that is serious business.

My favorite theme is grace, and the possibility that I might unintentionally imply there are limits on God's love deeply concerns me. However, I always try to remember that there's not a word in the definition of grace that implies indulgence, enabling, or "anything goes."

Grace is unconditional, undeserved, unlimited, unrelenting love—not undiscerning, unrestrained leniency.

Grace does not mean our behavior doesn't matter. Grace simply means that our worth in God's eyes and our place in his heart are not dependent on our behavior.[2]

But still . . . I always want to examine my motives and the potentially negative impact of my comments regarding divisive topics like this one. I don't want to make God's "love too narrow by false limits of my own."

IS THIS A "DISPUTABLE MATTER"?

Well, that's another complicated question. Ken Wilson pleads admirably for unity within the body of Christ, despite our different convictions on same-sex intimacy. He promotes a "third way approach"—one that moves beyond the division that arises when people migrate to the two extremes. Wilson asserts, "I think it is reasonable to regard this limited question—how the biblical prohibitions apply to monogamous gay relationships —as a 'disputable matter.'"[3]

Wilson appeals to Romans 14:1: "Accept the one whose faith is weak, without quarreling over disputable matters." He sees in that verse (and in the two chapters that follow it) the biblical instruction for congregations to hang together over matters that are not central to the gospel, and believes it is applicable in this conversation over sexuality.

I would absolutely agree that the topic of same-sex relation-ships is not central to the gospel. The Bible's teaching about homosexuality does not rise to the same level of paramount biblical teachings such as the resurrection of Jesus and salvation by grace through faith. Is same-sex sexual behavior, however, a "disputable matter"? Well, maybe it depends on how we define *disputable*.

Faithful Christians certainly do disagree over this matter, but that doesn't make it disputable. The disputable matters addressed in Romans 14 and 15 are diets and days. I don't mean to underestimate the tension in New Testament churches over what people ate and which days they considered holy, but I also don't believe they equal the gravity of sexual choices.

So is same-sex intimacy a disputable matter?

Well, one's stance on this is not a test of one's faith. There definitely can be people in the same faith communities who hold differing perspectives on this. Yet, it certainly is not a minor, unimportant, insignificant subject. This matter does matter.

PAINTING WITH AN UNWARRANTED BRUSH

It really complicates things when people get painted with an unwarranted brush. Note this declaration by John Shore, one who affirms same-sex intimacy:

> In recent years some Christian leaders have responded to the gay issue by making a ministry of "building bridges" between those who believe that being gay is a sin and those who don't. . . . I certainly understand how great that sounds.
>
> But it's not great. It doesn't even make sense. Because when it comes to the issue of LGBT equality, there is no middle ground. . . . The Christians on one side of this debate are claiming that, in the eyes of God, those on the other side are *less than human*. . . . No matter how strenuously he or she might deny it, any Christian who fails to forthrightly and unambiguously assert that there is nothing whatsoever inherently immoral about same-sex relationships has chosen a side in this conflict. They've chosen to perpetuate the maligning, ostracizing, and degradation of gay people by Christians.[4]

Phrases such as "there is no middle ground" and "building bridges doesn't even make sense" are not helpful. Lots of us want to nurture relationships across this divide. In fact, I would love to be part of bridge-building. I do not believe that articulating my beliefs invalidates or quashes such efforts.

Will these decisions result in divisions? Will denominations divide and will individual members choose to change churches over this? Of course. And understandably so. But the fact that people choose not to work together does not mean we can't see ourselves as brothers and sisters.

Moreover, I don't know any reasonable Christian who is claiming that same-sex attracted people are, as Shore charges, "less than human." It is irresponsible for Shore to make such claims about those who hold a Traditional view.

In all fairness, many writers on the Affirming side are not as harsh and belligerent as Shore. Writers such as Justin Lee (*Torn*), James Brownson (*Bible, Gender, Sexuality*), and Ken Wilson (*A Letter to My Congregation*) are much more conciliatory and more eager to find common ground.

I dislike the spirit I perceive behind Shore's ultimatum, but he is correct in asserting that this is such a hot-button topic, neutrality is not an option. We can build bridges and we can maintain loving relationships despite our disagreements. We cannot, however, wander aimlessly on this topic. Thinking Christians, particularly those in leadership, are going to have to decide what they believe about same-sex intimacy.

SPEAKING TO OUR YOUTH IS COMPLICATED TOO

If a church stays silent on this topic, its silence may encourage youth to experiment sexually, including the exploration of same-sex relationships. Unless the church offers a well-researched argument for the Traditional view, youth may not have motivation to pursue straight relationships. Scholar

Stanley Grenz quotes Fuller Seminary professor Don Williams: "For the church at this point to surrender to gay advocacy and gay theology . . . untold numbers of children and adolescents who are struggling with their sexual identity will conclude that 'gay is good,' deny their heterosexual potential and God's heterosexual purpose for them."[5] If there are teens who are struggling with their sexual identity, then a suggestion that they find their place in a same-sex relationship could be really attractive.

Ken Wilson reports the results of a study that found the following about churches taking a strong Traditional stance: "The kids kept their sexuality a secret from pastors and youth workers. Kids in these settings were at greater risk for self-harm, including suicide."[6] It is indeed alarming to consider the number of teens who sense a same-sex attraction, and perhaps act on that attraction, then harm themselves or retreat into a secret world due to shame heaped on them by peers and/or parents.

So there are two perspectives. The first perspective is, "If we don't take a stance, young people will be encouraged to experiment with same-sex relationships." The second perspective is, "If we do take a strong stance, youth will not ask for help and will dangerously internalize their struggles." Both of those viewpoints are legitimate. So what do we do?

Well, at the least these conflicting perspectives remind us to speak about this topic candidly, yet wisely and compassionately. We must not stifle honest questions and we must not speak to sexuality without doing our homework. We cannot merely tell teenagers how to behave; we have to equip them to think for themselves. We must love our youth enough to embrace them, to be honest with them about our own struggles, and to walk with them when they are grappling with sexual identity.

WHAT ABOUT LEGAL PROTECTION OF GAY PEOPLE?

This is a multifaceted conversation with history and legalities I don't understand. From what I know, however, it seems only fair and prudent to extend the legal privileges that straight people enjoy to those people who are in same-sex relationships. I'm talking about privileges that include everything from inheritance of estates to hospital visitation. Moreover, discrimination is unchristian, so we all should support the full recognition of a gay person's legal rights.

"JUDGE NOT" IS COMPLICATED

"Do not judge, or you too will be judged" (Jesus, quoted in Matthew 7:1). That might be one of the most quoted lines of our Lord. Yet, in the context of an act of sexual immorality committed by a Corinthian church member, 1 Corinthians 5:12-13 reads, "What business is it of mine to judge those outside the church? Are you not to judge those inside? God will judge those outside. 'Expel the wicked person from among you.'"

So what's the deal? Are we supposed to judge or are we not?

The Bible appears to say that, while God alone is in charge of judging those outside the church, those of us inside the church have a responsibility to hold each other accountable. Thus there seems to be a difference between judgmental attitudes toward those outside the Christian family and legitimate assessments within the family circle about what is right and wrong.

Now obviously the idea of holding each other accountable opens a can of dangerous worms, and 1 Corinthians 5:12-13 does not give us license to run around eagerly and arrogantly pointing out each other's sins. Yet there is a responsibility for honest and mature accountability within the Christian family.

So, let's take "judge not" seriously, but let's not take it further than it was intended. Judging is not the same as condemning. The Bible gives us a balance. That balance will be easier to maintain if we remember the lessons from the following examples.

My friend Barry Thomas and I went camping at Sherando Lake a few summers ago. It had been raining, and more rain was forecast, but we thought we could beat the odds.

After we set up our tents I was assigned the duty of gathering firewood. Unfortunately, everything was wet because of the rain. I gathered the driest wood I could find, but it wouldn't burn.

Barry was cooking dinner on the Coleman stove, but we wanted a campfire, so we decided I should drive about a mile back to the ranger shack to see if the rangers could point me to where I could buy firewood. On my way out of the campground I noticed another campsite from which campers had recently left and saw a hint of smoke rising from their campfire. "Well, that wood is dry," I said to myself. So I pulled in, grabbed a log by its cool end from the fire, and threw it into the back of my truck.

I drove the mile or so down to the ranger shack. When I stopped at the ranger shack I noticed an awful smell and saw smoke. "Oh, no!" I thought, "The ranger shack is on fire!" Then I looked into my rear view mirror . . . and it wasn't the ranger shack on fire. It was the log in the back of my truck!

As I was driving, the wind had ignited the embers of that log, and it was burning, along with part of the lining of the bed of my pickup! I put the fire out quickly, but the melted rubber in the lining of that pickup truck is still visible—a reminder of a day when I saw smoke and flames and assumed someone else had a real problem—when, in fact, *I* had a problem.

That blazing experience reminds me a little of one of the most unusual narratives in Scripture. In Genesis 38 we read that Judah was a good man, but he did a bad thing. Judah's beloved wife had died. On a trip out of town he hooked up with a woman he thought to be a prostitute. It turned out she was his widowed daughter-in-law Tamar. (I told you it is an odd story.) She was wearing a veil and perhaps it was dark because for some reason, he did not recognize her. So he slept with her, although, again, he didn't know it was his daughter-in-law. He must have left in a hurry, because he left some of his belongings behind.

Three months later, Judah found out that Tamar, his daughter-in-law, was pregnant. Not having any idea that it was his child, Judah was infuriated! Remember that she was a widow and, being unmarried, her pregnancy brought shame on Judah's family.

"Bring her out and have her burned to death!" Judah declared in Genesis 38:24 with what he probably would have described as righteous indignation. (And he had the power in that place and culture to do that.)

"As she was being brought out [for her execution], she sent a message to her father-in-law, 'I am pregnant by the man who owns these,' she said. And she added, 'See if you recognize whose seal and cord and staff these are'" (Genesis 38:25).

Judah's face must have turned ashen. He did recognize the items. They were his. He realized what he'd done. He had left them behind after his one night stand with the woman he thought . . . to this moment . . . was a prostitute. He now realized that the woman was Tamar. The child she carried was his.

A suddenly contrite Judah confessed, "She is more righteous than I" (Genesis 38:26) and called off her execution. Judah had seen smoke which he assumed was from someone else's fire . . . but the smoke was from his fire.

Judah was a good man, a man who loved God and hated evil. Yet Judah piously railed against the evil in another's life while conveniently ignoring the evil in his own.

Much like Judah, some high-profile critics of same-sex relationships have been discovered to be in secret, same-sex relationships themselves. In fact, it could be that some of the most strident critics are trying to suppress their own same-sex attractions. Debra Hirsch observed:

> Some of the most horrific acts of homophobic abuse have been at the hands of those who experience a form of "homosexual dread"—a fear of their own latent homosexuality. This is the only way one can understand fallen pastor Ted Haggard's homophobic vitriol, only to be found himself having a homosexual encounter.[7]

While I was writing this, a congressman who has championed the pro-life position and made it central to his campaigns resigned in disgrace after allegedly asking his pregnant mistress to get an abortion. Ted Haggard and Judah are not alone in their hypocrisy.

"Judge not" makes this conversation complicated.

WHEN YOUR CHILD IS GAY

Questions surrounding LGBT issues are difficult for Christian parents of gay sons and daughters. It's often messy and complicated when a son or daughter comes out.

Sometimes parents feel guilty. So many people have claimed that same-sex attraction is related to parental blunders that parents often ask, "What did I do wrong?" I hurt for parents who heap shame upon themselves, as if having a same-sex attracted son or daughter is something to be ashamed of or feel guilty for.

Sometimes parents (and other family members) wonder how to respond to their gay child's partner or wedding. One common question I get from aunts and uncles, grandparents, friends, and parents is, "Should I go to the wedding?" They love the person getting married, but they don't want to be perceived as endorsing same-sex marriage.

My counsel is always to err on the side of love. I understand the argument that attending a wedding is blessing the union. But I can't see the wisdom in risking damaged relationships with family members due to fear of what others think.

Sometimes parents are hurt by the insensitive comments of fellow Christians. I recoil at what people have said—sometimes innocently, sometimes not. We often hear, "Kids can be cruel." Well, adults can be cruel too—even Christian adults.

A mother and father of a gay daughter wrote this to me when their Traditional church was considering LGBT questions:

> We were surprised by our fellow church friends. Some hugged us close and supported us even if their opinions were different from ours. It was softly suggested by some that we might want to find another church. We overheard some very hateful conversations by other Christians. We had friends who were suddenly avoiding us. Some would turn their backs on us as they saw us approaching. It hurt deeply.

These hurtful comments are often condescending, such as, "God loves your child too." (As if the parent didn't know that already.) Or they are barbed with, "Didn't you raise them better than that?"

Sometimes parents of gay children leave their Traditional congregations to be part of church families that are Affirming. That usually comes with a feeling of great loss. But being around so many people, often long-time friends, who seem to feel their child is second class is just too much to take. These parents understand that not everyone in their church is judgmental and dismissive. Yet there are enough people who seem not to appreciate their sons and daughters for who they are that they long for a church family that is unequivocally supportive. Traditional churches often lose wonderful members because of insensitive ones.

One parent who holds a Traditional view once lamented that fellow Christians feel awkward around his daughter and others who are gay. He recognizes that his child needs relationships, and that the feeling of rejection sometimes drives gay Christians further away from the church. He longs for his Christian friends to love his daughter, even though he does not support his daughter's sexual choices.

Parents of gay sons and daughters need friends, not judges. They need invitations to dinner, but not evenings full of advice. They need help celebrating their sons and daughters, whether or not they affirm their sexual choices. And they need us to love their children unconditionally.

CHAPTER THREE

THE TERRIFYING BEAUTY OF A DIVERSE CHURCH OR DENOMINATION

HOW DO WE MOVE FORWARD? Can we avoid this difficult conversation? Should we? Is there a way to disagree without dividing? Has the potential for diverse families of faith gone the way of the political system—a system of extremes? Families of faith across the landscape are asking these critical questions.

IT'S PARTICULARLY DIFFICULT IF YOU ARE DIFFENDOOFERISH

Dr. Seuss's book *Hooray for Diffendoofer Day!* is a cute little story about a fun and creative place—Diffendoofer School in Dinkerville. One day, panic set in at Diffendoofer School. It looked like their small, diverse school might be shut down and they would have to go to school in Flobbertown.

"Not Flobbertown!" cried those who loved Dinkerville. "It's miserable in Flobbertown!" Flobbertown was known as the place where everyone dressed the same, thought the same, and would "march in single file." Flobbertown sounded awful to the students who liked the different ways of doing things at Diffendoofer School.[1]

Many churches and denominations are, let's say, rather homogenous. (I'd say they are a bit like Flobbertown, but that might not sound kind.) In many families of faith, the overwhelming majority of the people are either on the right end of the theological/political spectrum or on the left end of the theological/political spectrum.

Outliers within those homogenous congregations or denominations—those who find themselves clearly out-numbered—have learned to live with their minority status. They keep their nonconforming opinions to themselves. Because there are so many things about their family of faith that they like, they put up with those things they don't.

There are other congregations and denominations, however, which are politically and theologically diverse, much like the Diffendoofer School! Within such a family of faith one could find a variety of opinions on a variety of topics. Most members of such heterogeneous groups value the variety. Perhaps diversity of opinion is one of your faith community's niches in the kingdom. If so, that makes your faith community beautiful . . . and terrifying.

Serving Diffendooferish congregations seems to be my calling; I've served more than one of them. And I feel happily at home in such theological diversity.

One of the lessons I've learned about big tent churches is that no tent is big enough for everyone. Several years ago a couple who were members of the big tent church where I served at that time came to my office and took a seat on the couch. "Travis," they told me, "We love this church, and we're not mad, but this church is becoming too liberal on the topic of women in ministry." They were polite and complimentary, but they moved their membership to a more conservative church.

Six weeks later—and I'm not making this up—a family came to my office. Sitting on the same couch, they said, "Travis, we love this church, and we're not mad, but we think this church and this denomination is too conservative on the topic of sexuality." They were gracious, and yet they went to a more progressive church in another denomination.

While I hated to see both families go, I understand that no tent can hold everyone. Any church or denomination that tries to be all things to all people will lose its identity, focus, and mission. Given that reality, however, I have learned it is possible for people with a wide variety of perspectives on important issues to remain within their family of faith.

LESSONS FROM THE COUNCIL OF JERUSALEM

At the time there was only one church in the world—the first ever church—the church in Jerusalem. Then up in Antioch some people who had migrated from Jerusalem started a different kind of church doing different kinds of things reaching different kinds of people. Since the good folks back in Jerusalem knew only one model of church, all those differences became the source of conflict.

Those differences included the evangelization of Gentiles, including different ethnic groups. More importantly, the Christians in Antioch were not following all the traditions that the Christians in Jerusalem believed were so important. It all came to a head when self-appointed representatives of the Jerusalem church went to Antioch and declared, "You can't do all these different things! And let's start with circumcision. Where did you get the idea you people don't have to be circumcised? You can't be a Christian without it! Everybody knows that."

The conflict was so severe, people of Antioch and Jerusalem had to have the Council of Jerusalem. James, the leader of the Jerusalem church and whose authority was respected in Antioch, listened carefully to the lengthy debate and eventually stated, "This is how it's going to be." He made a list of compromises, saving the relationship between those two churches and shaping the future of all churches. (You can read the story in Acts 15.) Here are some lessons we can learn from our ecclesiastical ancestors.

Sometimes even churches need to have hard conversations and make difficult decisions. Had the leaders of the Jerusalem church suffered from an unhealthy aversion to conflict they would have kicked this can down the road. They would have hemmed, and they would have hawed. They might even have said, "Our annual stewardship emphasis is coming up, and we don't want to rock the boat!" But they wisely understood that even churches have to have hard conversations. The harmony of the church of Jerusalem was risked temporarily so that the mission of the church might be enriched permanently.

Conflict handled well can be good for an organization. An old saying reminds us, "When two partners always agree, one of them is unnecessary." Conflict helps everyone look at the matter in a new way. Conflict, rightly handled, forces us to see things from new angles. George W. Bullard even wrote a book titled *Every Congregation Needs a Little Conflict.*

The Jerusalem congregation was stronger for having faced the matter head on. They learned how to handle conflict well, and the tension between the two camps resulted in a healthy blend of tradition and innovation.

When considering complex matters, sometimes the best we can do is say, "it seems." In Acts 15:28 there is a fascinating line: "It seemed good to the Holy Spirit and to us." *Seemed.* I'd never paid attention to that word *seemed* until Pastor John Ortberg pointed it out in his book *All the Places to Go . . . How Will You Know?*[2]

This was a historic moment. The Christian movement was in its infancy. The second church in history had been birthed out of the first church in history. Their decisions would affect not only those two original churches but also all churches. You and I never have been in a business meeting or church conference of such importance as this one. They were shaping the future.

And the best they could come up with was, "It seemed."

Often, in dealing with complex topics, the best we can do is to say, "It seems." This issue in Jerusalem was challenging —a clash of values—and a difficult conversation involving 1,500 years of tradition. They were having that conversation without benefit of the New Testament and without decades of experience with church matters.

Theirs was an attempt to balance what they understood to be truth with what they had experienced as grace. As fallible human beings, they could not honestly declare they had arrived at the one, definitive, end-all-discussion, Christian answer. But they could in all honesty say, "This is the best decision that can be made. It seems to us that this is the right thing. This is our best attempt at balancing grace and truth."

I hope those who "won" (and I use that term loosely) didn't gloat or disparage those who disagreed with the final decision. And I hope those who disagreed with the final decision understood the reasoning of James, believed they'd been heard, and still felt like they had a place at the table. After all, the church leaders were simply doing their best, as finite humans, to address a thorny topic. Sound familiar?

Scholar John Stackhouse, in discussing the role of women in ministry, offered an observation that is helpful to our discussion on sexuality:

> Our task as theologians—and, indeed, the task of any responsible Christian—is to do the best we can to understand the Word of God in its multifarious complexity,

even though that will sometimes result in an interpretation that does not fit every piece of the puzzle together without strain.[3]

We can unashamedly acknowledge that no one in this discussion is going to have an airtight argument. But it is possible to say, with integrity and defensible reason, "It seems."

To admit that the best we can do is "It seems" is not to say we do not have convictions on the topic. The leaders of the Jerusalem church declared "It seems" and then took a position. They did not throw up their hands in acquiescence to uncertainty.

When I say "It seems" and then declare my conviction about same-sex relationships, what I mean is this: my understanding of the Bible will not allow me to be neutral on this matter. However, I acknowledge that all of us see through a glass darkly, and so I grant respect to those I disagree with. The convictions I express here are convictions I hold deeply, though I acknowledge that my interpretation does not "fit every piece of the puzzle together without strain."[4] Therefore, I stand here firmly. But I stand here humbly.

People who differed chose to work together, because there was a place in God's mission to fill. So, did everyone in Jerusalem change their minds after the pronouncement of James? Highly unlikely. There were almost certainly post-meeting analyses in the parking lot. There were almost certainly some people who doubted the wisdom of the decision. Some almost certainly questioned James's leadership.

But there was a world to reach and a church to build. They would be neither blind to their differences, nor hamstrung by their differences. They could not afford to gloss over the issue and could not afford to obsess over the issue.

When I was pastor of the Lucas Grove Baptist Church near Upton, Kentucky, we celebrated our ninetieth anniversary. In preparation, I waded through the records of the church looking for stories. One of my favorite stories came from the days when the first church house was being built back in 1896. In that year, Jim Scaggs was a little boy attending the Lucas Grove School, which sat next to the land where the Lucas Grove Baptist Church was being built. Scaggs later wrote in church records that during school he would sit and look out the window, watching church members working on the building. When he wrote about watching them build the church he made special note of the fact that some of the workers had on silver hats and some had on gold ones.

Why was it noteworthy that people with silver hats and people with gold hats were working together? In 1896 there was a bitterly contested presidential election between William McKinley (Republican) and William Jennings Bryan (Democrat). The country was struggling economically and there was a rancorous debate over whether US currency would be based on silver or gold. Democrats said silver. Republicans said gold. It was a nasty division, much like the division caused by the explosive social issues of our day. The silver versus gold argument split friends and families, and people wore hats to boldly declare which side they were on.

But there they were—people who felt so strongly about the issue that they came wearing either a gold or silver hat—sawing and hammering, handing each other tools and lumber, working side by side to build a church. Here were people who felt strongly about a dispute that could have divided them . . . yet who felt *more* strongly about the mission that united them.

And it made a lasting impression on a little boy. Doesn't that sound like a great church?!

EUODIA AND SYNTYCHE

There is another story from the early church that can help us with our diverse families of faith: the disagreement between Euodia and Syntyche found in Philippians 4. We don't know the exact nature of the conflict, yet it seems pretty clear that the disagreement between these two women is at the heart of the church-wide tension that Paul addresses off and on throughout his letter to the Philippians.

Euodia and Syntyche must have had influence in the church, as Paul says they had worked alongside him in the cause of the gospel. Perhaps their argument was over leadership—which one of them would occupy the highest place in the church's pecking order. We don't know the nature of their dispute, but we do know that God inspired Paul to write that these two leaders in the church should "be of the same mind" (Philippians 4:2). Does this suggest that Euodia and Syntyche should think the same thing? It's hard to imagine we are expected to think these two women were supposed to, somehow, think exactly alike. So what does "of the same mind" mean?

Maybe Paul meant they should have the same mind as Jesus. Perhaps he was not saying at all that they should think the same thing. It might be that he was remembering what he wrote earlier in his letter to the Philippians: "Have the same mindset as Christ Jesus" (Philippians 2:5). Then he went on to talk about the servant nature of Jesus' incarnation. Maybe Euodia and Syntyche were not supposed to agree on everything but rather were supposed to defer to each other, following the model of Jesus.

Maybe Paul was talking about harmony, not unanimity. In the New American Standard Bible, Philippians 4:2 reads, "I urge Euodia and I urge Syntyche to live in harmony in the Lord." Dissonance is when two different notes make the other sound worse. Harmony is when two different notes make the other sound better. Two people can have diverse opinions, but if their hearts are right toward each other, their differences can sound like harmony, not dissonance.

Maybe Paul meant they should be willing to stretch (and I do think that's what he meant). I believe God was saying to them, through Paul, "You need to stretch your minds in the direction of the other. Be willing to consider her point of view. Move as far as you can in the direction of the opposing view."

I'm afraid lots of us are unwilling to think differently about anything. We tend to watch the TV channels and read the books and listen to the commentators who reinforce what we think. And yet those of us in diverse families of faith will have to stretch (or, as we like to say in our church, "s-t-r-e-t-c-h"). We can "be of the same mind" even if we don't agree on everything if we are willing to stretch in the direction of those we disagree with.

"SHOULD I STAY OR SHOULD I GO?"

People who find themselves in the minority within their church or denomination, especially when the topic in question is important to them, face a difficult decision—should I stay or should I go?

I believe the default answer is to stay.

The missionary Paul began his letter to his protégé Timothy with an interesting mandate: "As I urged you when I went into Macedonia, stay there in Ephesus" (1 Timothy 1:3). Perhaps

Timothy had expressed openly to Paul his desire to move to greener pastures—to go to an easier assignment where the people were better humored. But Paul said, "Timothy, you stay in Ephesus."

Leaving is awfully tempting sometimes. People who too easily walk away from tough situations, however, never experience the satisfaction that comes on the other side of hard conversations, and they have little positive impact on anybody.

A few years ago, the pastor of the East Waynesville Baptist Church in Waynesville, North Carolina, said the church was going to become politically active, and if folks weren't in agreement with him regarding politics then they knew where to find the door. Well, all heck broke out, the national media found out, and the building was packed during a called business meeting. In a room filled with cameras and thick with tension, the pastor surprised everyone by resigning.

When the pastor walked out, his supporters stormed out. "I resign all my positions!" shouted one. Others yelled out scathing accusations against those still seated. Those who had believed the pastor was abusing his authority and taking the church down a dangerous path, most of them long-term members, remained inside. People sat quietly until a man went to the piano and began to play. Eventually Deacon Frank Lowe stood before the members and said, "If you've ever been loyal to your church, this is the time."[5]

There are several morals of this story, but the most important for our purposes here is the plea from Deacon Lowe: "If you've ever been loyal to your church, this is the time."

I told that story to our church during our discussion about sexuality and the Bible. I also encourage you to remember that story if you are thinking about leaving your church (or denomination) over the conversation about sexuality. If you've ever been loyal to your church, this is the time to be so. Never will your congregation need your loyalty more than during hard conversations over sexuality.

A seat at a diverse table requires a commitment. A commitment to each other. A commitment to the holiness to which we all are called. And a commitment to remain at the table when the family needs to make a decision and our opinion does not prevail.

SOMETIMES, HOWEVER . . .

It would be naive of me to assume people can remain as part of a church (or denomination) when that body has violated their convictions. Convictions are deeply held, firm, grounded, defensible, and defining beliefs. Thus people sometimes find it impossible to remain in a family of faith whose positions are profoundly different from their own.

Decisions like that are best reached, however, with an understanding that, as the saying goes, every hill is not worth dying on. People in healthy, diverse churches understand that everyone is in the minority over something. People in healthy, diverse churches are willing to move as far in the direction of the opposing position as they can without violating their consciences.

Nevertheless, in the end, the differences are sometimes just too great. Sometimes leaving is the right choice. Sometimes people have to leave for the sake of their emotional health. Sometimes they choose to leave so as not to cause further damage to the family of faith they love. Sometimes the dissonance between their personal convictions and the decision of the majority is so uncomfortable that it's simply best to choose another place to serve. Leaving is never the best *first* option, but sometimes leaving is the best *final* option.

WHAT ABOUT DENOMINATIONS?

With denominations, the relationships are not as intimate as in local churches. The connections are not so tight. So, loyalty to one's denomination is not usually as compelling as loyalty to one's local church family.

Nevertheless, a number of local congregations and pastors have chosen to remain in their denominations despite differences with the majority. One argument given for remaining is that changes at the denominational level actually don't change many things at the local level. Local folks argue, "Edicts and pronouncements originating from some meeting far away have little direct impact on us. We're still going to be who we are." Church members say, "We're going to keep on doing church like we've always done it, no matter what declarations they make in the denominational offices." (That's a naïve assumption, by the way, and we'll talk about that momentarily.) So they stay.

Others simply believe the mission they share with their denominational family trumps the beliefs they don't. So they remain in the fold for the sake of educational institutions, justice initiatives, and social ministries. They stay for the sake of missionaries across the globe whose support they share. Missional cooperation, for many, is simply a higher value than doctrinal conformity.

Another common reason for staying in a denomination is to remain a prophetic voice from within. People who have deep ties to a national body are often not content to write off that body. They become loyal dissenters. Often their opposition is gentle, well-reasoned, and respectful, though sometimes their opposition is emotional and strident. (My hunch is some denominational leaders would breathe a sigh of relief if a few of their congregations would go ahead and withdraw.)

Some congregations, obviously, make the terribly difficult decision to leave their denominational family. Longstanding relationships are fractured. Facebook feuds abound. In some cases, arguments and lawsuits over who owns the buildings consume a painful amount of time and money.

So why would a church leave its denomination over the matter of sexuality? For many, this is a defining issue. This is not one of those marginal debates about which disagreement is justifiable. And for many, being labeled as either liberals or fundamentalists (depending on where they lie on their denomination's spectrum) by their denominational partners has grown tiresome. Some people are weary, as a friend of mine put it, of having adversaries from within their denominations constantly "in their grill." This fight has been exhausting for lots of people, and many feel the energy spent debating this topic would be better spent on evangelism and meeting human needs. So some have withdrawn from the fray.

Many also recognize that, while a denomination's decision might not make an immediate difference in a local congregation, in time the impact inevitably will be felt. Such realities as the theological bent of ministers coming out of the denomination's seminaries and the positions championed by denominational literature eventually do have an impact on local churches. Insightful people at the local church level understand that, although they do not feel an immediate impact from denominational decisions, down the road they likely will. The church will notice that pastors coming from the denomination's seminaries have different theological views than previous graduates, and they will notice that the Sunday school and discipleship literature has a different slant than before. So, recognizing that changes at the denominational level eventually do trickle down to the local church level, congregations sometimes decide to leave.

Moreover, many recognize that a denomination's decision cannot be divorced from the national debate on this topic. A denomination's stated position sends a signal to society-at-large as to where people of that denomination stand on that question. Outsiders tend to lump together all who are identified by a denominational label. Outsiders often do not recognize the diversity that can exist among congregations and individuals within a denominational family.

Those who believe the denomination has veered from its historic identity are thus placed in a difficult position. Local churches may seek a formal way to distance themselves from the denomination's stance. Not to demonize the denomination, but to say, "This decision is beyond the lines. That's not who we are." And the only way to distance themselves might be to disaffiliate.

One of the most trying scenarios occurs when a congregation is no longer welcome around the denominational table. There are occasions when the larger group believes a local congregation has violated the shared values of the denominational body, and so barring the congregation from the larger group is justified. Such removals from the fellowship can be painful for the local church and for the denomination, and the media often exacerbate the pain of separation.

It's hard to imagine how negatively our constant dividing into smaller and smaller groups must be perceived by unchurched people. Yet, as with Paul and Barnabas, sometimes good people view things so differently that separation is the only viable option.

It's easy to pity denominational executives nowadays. Across the board, denominational participation is plummeting and bank accounts are dwindling. The very purpose and future of denominations are in question. The last thing denominational leaders need is a brouhaha over sexuality.

Good denominational leaders are now torn between doctrinal soundness and open-hearted inclusiveness, between the influence of the large congregations and the rights of the smaller ones. Understandably and inevitably, the need for funding is always part of the equation. These denominational executives are, after all, charged with the mission and future of their denominations.

Ministry in the context of the same-sex debate presents unprecedented challenges to organizational relationships. Some denominations identify as *connectional*, meaning that every congregation is part of a formal network, and the connection is both defined and part of the congregation's identity. Other congregations identify as *congregational*, meaning the churches are autonomous and cooperate with others in their denomination only to whatever level they believe to be appropriate.

Churches that are connectional will have less flexibility at the local level than congregational churches. The challenge of connectional churches will be how to influence their denomination and then, if they find themselves out of step with their denomination, how to disengage from the denomination then connect with like-minded congregations of their denominational tradition. This desire to link themselves with like-minded congregations, of course, often results in the formation of new denominations that identify with their heritage yet distinguish themselves from others who find their identity in that same heritage, such as Presbyterian congregations that break away from their historic denominational identity to form a new denomination, thus linking up with like-minded Presbyterians, and so on.

THE MEANING OF CONVICTIONS

One word that gets used a lot in this conversation is *conviction*. As I said above, people don't want to violate their convictions. And understandably so.

However, sometimes I wonder if we might be using that word *conviction* a bit loosely. When we do that, the ability to participate in a diverse family of faith is minimized. Given the possibility that some of us are using *conviction* sloppily, I'm including some thoughts about convictions.

- A conviction is not merely a preference.
- A conviction is not merely an opinion.
- A conviction is not merely an assumption.
- A conviction is not merely a presupposition.
- A conviction is deeply held. Firm. Grounded.

Conviction is rooted in the Latin word for *convince*. Thus, a conviction is not something we've been told is true, have always assumed to be true, or something we judged to be true without considering evidence. People who hold a true conviction are able to give a reasonable explanation as to what convinced them.

We don't have to have convictions about every topic, by the way. There is no shame in holding a mere opinion about something, or in merely stating an inclination.

It is hard to imagine a thinking Christian not having at least an informed opinion on the topic at hand. And I do believe vocational ministers should have a clear and well-thought-out position on the same-sex topic because of the responsibility for theological leadership that comes with our calling. Nevertheless, it is not a sign of spiritual or intellectual weakness for anyone to say, "It seems to me," instead of, "It is my firm conviction."

So let's not confuse preferences, opinions, assumptions, and presuppositions with convictions. Convictions are those deeply held, firm, grounded, defensible beliefs that define us. They shape our worldview and thus determine the trajectory of our lives.

Churches who thrive despite their diversity understand the value of wide-ranging preferences and opinions. They grant grace to each other regarding even their assumptions and presuppositions, recognizing that we all have them. They refuse to fragment over non-essentials, and they recognize a shorter list of essentials than others do. In a big tent church, for example, everyone is in the minority over something.

True, sometimes people of conviction find it impossible to remain in a church (or denomination) whose positions are deeply different from their own. Painful divisions over diverging convictions are understandable, though deeply regrettable. What is even more regrettable, however, is that some churches divide over mere opinions and preferences. When we have a conviction it is indeed dishonorable not to defend it, even contend for it. The mistake comes in labeling something a conviction that does not deserve that weighty description.

───

Those among us who long for unity—who would give just about anything if we could all just get along—must be terribly discouraged by the depth of our divisions. Yet, as we move now to an exploration of the topic itself, it becomes apparent (however regrettable) why we are so polarized.

PART TWO

THE TOPIC

CHAPTER FOUR

THE AFFIRMING POSITION

LET'S TURN OUR ATTENTION to the Christian case for committed, monogamous, covenant-based same-sex relationships, including same-sex marriage (the Affirming position).

Through the years and in various settings, people have known my Traditional view of sexuality, yet I believe people have found me to be conciliatory in my relationships and considerate of diverse opinions. In the following chapter I want to be respectful of and accurately represent the opposing point of view.

I intentionally use the words committed, monogamous, and covenant-based here because no responsible Christian supports sexual promiscuity. People represented here contend for committed partnerships. They are not advocating a multi-partnered, unrestrained, sex-for-fun lifestyle. They are defending lifelong covenants, whether the couples are straight or gay. Professor David Gushee advocates for "celibacy outside of lifetime covenantal marriage, monogamous fidelity within lifetime covenantal marriage" for both gay and straight couples.[1] Author Matthew Vines also believes the church should support and affirm the "God-reflecting covenant" between same-sex couples. Vines goes so far as to say that not to affirm such relationships is sin: "So it isn't gay Christians who are sinning against God by entering into monogamous, loving relationships. It is the church that is sinning against them by rejecting their intimate relationships."[2]

So why do some Christians affirm the legitimacy of committed same-sex relationships? What is their motivation? What is the reasoning behind their advocacy of same-sex marriage? Some Traditionalists even ask, "How could a Christian affirm same-sex intimacy?"

The following are what I perceive to be the most common reasons given by Christians who affirm and support same-sex sexual relations. I will do my best to allow those in the Affirming camp to speak for themselves, so you will find several quotations here.

THE BIBLE CONDEMNS EXPLOITATIVE SEX, NOT MONOGAMOUS, COMMITTED SAME-SEX RELATIONSHIPS

We begin with the most common argument among Christians for the legitimacy of same-sex intimacy: the same-sex behavior prohibited in Scripture is that of exploitative sex (i.e., pederasty, same-sex prostitution, or sex slavery), not the monogamous, committed same-sex relationships we know today. Matthew Vines, for example, says, "Like most theologically conservative Christians, I hold what is often called a 'high view' of the Bible." Yet Vines goes on to declare that "some parts of the Bible address cultural norms that do not directly apply to modern societies."[3]

The most common explanation by those who believe in Scripture's authority yet advocate for same-sex relationships is that the writers of the Bible knew nothing of the devoted, mutual, lifetime gay relationships that we know today. Those in the Affirming camp suggest that the Bible's prohibitions are against sex slavery, male temple prostitution, pederasty (adult men having sex with boys), and/or the depravity of the Roman emperors that included unrestrained sex with both women and men or boys. Therefore, they contend, we cannot say that the Bible and the historic church have condemned the faithful relationships between same-sex attracted people that are being advocated for in our day and time. I'll include here a few examples of those who make that argument.

Pastor Colby Martin is one of many who has determined that the nature of same-sex relationships in the ancient Greco-Roman world was not the same as faithful relationships we know today. He explains his understanding of the biblical texts: "There was no box for the category of a loving, committed, mutually respecting (and nonexploitative) same-sex relationship. . . . [Paul was condemning] activities like keeping young boys as sex-slaves, engaging in prostitution, and pagan idol-worship orgies."[4]

Pastor John Shore put it like this:

> We can be confident that Paul was not writing to, or about, gay people, because he simply *could not have been*, any more than he could have written about smartphones, iPads, or televisions. We do not know what Paul might write or say today about gay people. . . . Christians, therefore, have no Bible-based moral justification to condemn such acts.[5]

A closely related argument is articulated well by Professor James V. Brownson, who contends that the New Testament's condemnation of homosexuality, particularly in Romans 1, is actually the renouncement of out-of-control lust, not the prohibition of covenant love among gay people. Brownson theorizes that in Romans 1, Paul "describes same-sex eroticism as 'consumed with passion' (1:27) and as an expression of the 'lusts of their hearts' (1:24)," and that Paul "has in view an expression of intense or excessive desire."[6]

Thus, Brownson's argument goes, gay or lesbian couples who are married (or, where that is not possible, are in a covenant, exclusive relationship) are not guilty of the irresponsible excesses condemned in Romans 1. Therefore, Romans 1 does not directly condemn such covenant relationships between people of the same sex.

To summarize, many Affirmers believe the Bible condemns exploitative, abusive, and irresponsible same-sex relationships, but not the monogamous, covenantal relationships so common today in our society.

THE BIBLE NEEDS UPDATING

Many of those on the Affirming side of things acknowledge the Bible's denunciation of same-sex intimacy. They simply appeal to our reason and our relationships and suggest that our twenty-first-century insights trump the teaching of Scripture. We have to take into consideration, many Affirmers say, what we have learned since the days in which the Bible was written.

William Loader is one who believes the Bible teaches what we would call a Traditional view of sexuality. Loader clearly believes the Bible forbids same-sex intimacy. Yet, he also suggests we need "to update biblical writers' understanding and assumptions and respectfully acknowledge that their witness, which we treasure and in which we hear the word of God, was expressed in the language and thought-world of its time."[7] And, Loader posits further that "it has been necessary to supplement first-century understandings of reality with twenty-first-century understandings."[8] He explains that "to truly honor Scripture and respect Paul, we do better to acknowledge respectfully that we see Paul's understanding of human sexuality as no longer adequate."[9]

The late Walter Wink was another Christian academician who was willing to say the Bible doesn't have the last word on this matter. He was an influential religious scholar, and his position on this matter is often noted. In an article titled "Biblical Perspectives on Homosexuality" that appeared in *Christian Century* way back in 1979, Wink acknowledged that "the Bible clearly considers homosexuality a sin, and whether it is stated three times or 3,000 is beside the point. . . . The issue is precisely whether that biblical judgment is correct."[10] Wink went on to say that the Bible's position on such matters as slavery and divorce give us cause not to trust the Bible's accuracy on ethical matters.

Episcopal bishop John S. Spong likewise acknowledges the Bible's disapproval of same-sex intimacy and simply disagrees with the Bible. Spong says, "Even with the context explained and the words analyzed, it still appears to me that Paul would not approve of homosexual behavior."[11]

Bishop Spong contends, however, that Paul's opinion about homosexuality was simply inaccurate, for Paul did not have the information that you and I have. He asks, "Is Paul's commentary on homosexuality more absolute than some of his other antiquated, culturally conditioned ideas?" and later refers to "Paul's ill-informed, culturally biased prejudices."[12] Paul's opinion, therefore, is not to be equated with divine revelation.

I disagree with Loader, Wink, and Spong. We view the inspiration of Scripture very differently. Yet I do find their candor refreshing. Instead of trying to reinterpret Scripture to fit their viewpoint, they openly acknowledge that Scripture disapproves of same-sex sexual behavior and boldly say, "Let's not play games about what the Bible teaches; let's simply acknowledge that we have a broader and deeper understanding of sexuality today than its writers did."

Then there are those who advocate for committed same-sex relationships based not primarily on biblical exegesis but on relationships. Their positions grow out of their relationships with same-sex attracted people. For example, Gushee writes,

> My mind has changed—especially due to the transformative encounters I have been blessed to have with gay, lesbian, bisexual and transgender Christians over the last decade. One of them is my own beloved sister, who is dearer to me than words can say and who came out as a lesbian not long ago.[13]

A large number of people would say they support same-sex relationships because they have observed good fruit in the relationships of committed, Christian gay couples, and what they have observed has caused them to rethink their understanding of the Scriptures.[14]

Minds have been changed by hearts.

An interesting debate is whether or not a close relationship with someone who is gay is helpful in reaching the most "Christian" conclusion on this topic. It could be argued that, when one has a close relationship with a same-sex attracted person, what one gains in empathy one loses in objectivity. Of course it could also be argued that a close relationship with a gay person offers insights that are impossible without such a relationship.

So, to recap, one of the most popular thoughts behind the affirmation of faithful same-sex relationships is that our reason and relationships tell us that the Bible's teaching on same-sex relationships is not applicable in today's context.

THE CHURCH'S REPUTATION
AND FUTURE ARE IN JEOPARDY

One of the reasons why some encourage the church to advocate for same-sex partnerships is that they are concerned for the future of the church. They believe that if we oppose same-sex marriage and disapprove of same-sex intimacy we are going to lose lots of people, especially young adults. They note that evangelicals are widely viewed as judgmental, pharisaical, and closed-minded. (Indeed, every survey I've seen reflects the majority perception of the church by outsiders that we are intensely anti-gay.) Thus we are losing lots of people who are choosing to distance themselves from the church. A fear for the church's future causes many to say we cannot afford to alienate so many people over this issue, and therefore we must take a more progressive stance.

IT'S HYPOCRITICAL TO RAIL AGAINST SAME-SEX RELATIONSHIPS BUT BE SOFT ON DIVORCE

A number of people have countered the Traditionalist position with the charge that the church has chosen to be soft on divorce and tough on same-sex relationships. The former, they argue, is wreaking more havoc on the American family than the latter.

We have made concessions to divorced couples in our churches, it is suggested, so why aren't we making similar concessions to people in same-sex relationships? Ken Wilson declared, "I couldn't shake the thought that if we applied the same pastoral consideration to gay people that we give to the divorced and remarried, we'd come up with something much different than the categorical exclusions from church and ministry that we have practiced."[15]

This is a common charge, and one which gives reason for pause. After all, there is a lot more divorce of straight couples than marriage of gay couples. The following satirical quote from Greg Boyd arrested me and forced me to think deeply about my approach to this and other moral issues:

We evangelicals may be divorced and remarried several times; we may be as greedy and as unconcerned about the poor and as gluttonous as others in our culture; we may be as prone to gossip and slander and as blindly prejudiced as others in our culture; we may be more self-righteous and as rude as others in our culture—we may even lack love more than others in the culture. These sins are among the most frequently mentioned sins in the Bible. But at least we're not gay![16]

USING THE BIBLE TO OPPOSE SAME-SEX INTIMACY IS SIMILAR TO USING IT TO SUPPORT SLAVERY

Those on the Affirming side often declare that the use of the Bible to oppose same-sex sexual behavior is reminiscent of the use of the Bible to support slavery. Admittedly, lots of Americans used the Bible to justify slavery. That's a fact and, of course, that was one of the darkest chapters of our nation's history. Advocates of an Affirming position often see using the Bible to oppose same-sex intimacy as the same kind of proof-texting (picking and choosing fragments of Scripture to prove a point) that our predecessors were guilty of in justifying slavery.

JESUS DOESN'T MENTION SAME-SEX INTIMACY, AND THE BIBLE SAYS LITTLE

There are only a few biblical texts that speak directly to same-sex intimacy, and there is no record of Jesus mentioning it. If this were a major issue, it is argued, the Bible would have dedicated more ink to it. Jesus certainly would have said something about it if it were important. Shore put it like this: "The fact that homosexuality is so rarely mentioned in the Bible should be an indication to us of the lack of importance ascribed to it by the authors of the Bible."[17]

LOVE SHOULD BE OUR MESSAGE

The broader witness of Scripture tells us that God is love. Therefore, the argument goes that love should be our message, not a narrow morality. This concept of the broader witness of Scripture is a common defense of same-sex intimacy. The idea is that selected, isolated sections of Scripture must not be interpreted in such a way as to contradict the overarching themes of the Bible, such as grace and justice (fairness). Opposition to same-sex relationships is seen as hurtful to people, judgmental, and narrow, and thus as not reflecting the gracious nature of God depicted in the broad sweep of Holy Scripture.

Indeed, a solid principle of biblical interpretation is that obscure instructions should be interpreted in light of broader themes, and that more clearly understandable texts shed crucial light on the less understandable ones. Thus, advocates of an Affirming position appeal to the bigger witness—the recurring theme—of grace within Scripture. They believe a non-Affirming posture violates the Bible's emphasis on grace.

THE EARLY CHURCH INCLUDED GENTILES

Those on the Affirming side declare that we should follow the lead of the early church, for they included the Gentiles. Theologian Mark Achtemeier is one who sees the inclusion of Gentiles in the early church, as recorded in Acts, as justification for the inclusion of gay people in today's church. He suggests that the Jews felt toward the Gentiles like many church people feel toward same-sex attracted people. Yet, Achtemeier notes, "When the Gentiles come into the church, there is *no* requirement for them to repent of being Gentiles. These new believers remain who they are."[18]

Achtemeier, like many others, sees the inclusion of Gentiles as a precedent and validation for the full and unrestricted inclusion of same-sex attracted persons in the life of the church, although their marriages and relationships are outside traditional understanding of the Bible's message.

TRADITIONALISTS SIMPLY DESIRE TO MAINTAIN THE STATUS QUO

Those on the Affirming side declare that opposition to same-sex relationships results from unrecognized fear and a blindness to our desire to maintain our status (and the status quo). Read these words from Bishop Spong, and see if any part of his statement might ring true:

> Those who possess power define those who are powerless and then impose their own definition on the ones defined. The guiding principle is to ensure the comfort, the convenience, the happiness, and the well-being of the dominant ones. . . .
>
> Behind prejudice there is also fear. We reject that which we cannot manage. We condemn what we do not understand.[19]

Spong clearly hypothesizes that those who oppose same-sex intimacy merely want to hold on to the majority position of power enjoyed by straight people. Furthermore, Spong would suggest, we have said for so long that God only approves of straight relationships that we actually have convinced one another that it is true (whether it is or not).

Whether or not we agree with Spong's position on same-sex sexual practice (and I don't), his charges demand honest introspection from us.

I hope those who question the logic of the Affirming position see that the position is not without its solid arguments. I hope

Traditionalists who question the motivation of those who take a non-Traditional stance will see their hearts. I hope anyone who has said, "No true Christian could advocate for same-sex marriage" will say that no longer.

TESTIMONIAL

FROM A LESBIAN CHRISTIAN

Below is a testimonial from a close friend who happens to be a lesbian. We have a long-term, honest, and mutually respectful relationship despite our obvious disagreements. Although I'd be honored to have her in the congregation I serve, she would not feel fully welcomed there due to our church's recent position statement that would limit her leadership opportunities.

I include her testimonial simply because I believe voices like hers deserve to be heard. I spend a good part of this book offering a very different perspective from what you will read in this testimonial. However, I respect my friend, and we always have valued each other's candor.

When I hear the negative comments from the Christian leaders regarding gay people and how they feel about them and their "lifestyle choices" and "sin," it is hurtful to not only me but my friends as well. We are real people with real feelings, and they know nothing about me or how I live my life; they just seem to judge me because of who I love and want to spend the rest of my life with, regardless of the rest of who I am and what I do. That seems unfair and not at all Christian. I live my life by the Ten Commandments, and none of them say, "Thou shalt not be gay." If I can say I live by those rules in my life, how can an earthly representative of the church stand up and condemn me?

I want to be received just as anyone else would want to be received: open and able to be fully engaged. I am a lesbian; that is just a piece of who I am. I am Christian too; that is also just a piece of who I am. I should not be defined wholly by who I am married to, or treated any differently than any other person visiting or wanting to join a church. My relationship with God is no different from anyone else's, and because of that I need to be looked at by the church as an active member with my family equal to all other members of the church. The church is not here to judge; I should be welcomed.

Growing up in a traditional Southern Baptist church gave me some of the best times of my life. Playing in the choir room with my grandmother as she got ready for Sunday service and vacation Bible school with my friends are some of my fondest memories. The music, the always-fresh altar flowers, and the sense of community and belonging are part of what I remember as my church experience. As I grew up and away from the church, these were the memories I kept in my heart. When I came out as a lesbian and realized my church was not welcoming of me or my family, I did seek out alternative churches and services. None of them gave me the same feeling that I got from the traditional service and music I remembered; those services and churches were not for me. I wanted a traditional service in a traditional church as I remembered. We have landed in the Episcopalian church. It seems to fill our spiritual needs and is very welcoming of me, my wife, and our girls as a family—not just as individuals. I still long for the traditional Baptist service and beautiful choirs, but I will not compromise who I am for that—the tradeoff is just too dangerous.

Welcoming but Not Affirming sounds good at first, especially when you think of the church as not welcoming at all. Then it starts to settle on you what it means, and you think that is not welcoming at all. It sounds like, "You can come here and we will be nice to you but we don't want to know that you are married to a woman," or maybe it means, "We are okay knowing you are married to a woman, but you cannot fully engage in the church even as members, because we are going to talk about your sin and judge it." I remember my conversation with Travis, and he explained that even as a member of the church, it would be unlikely that I would be able to hold certain leadership positions in his church. He said that I would be not seen as someone who could represent the church; that his church could no more have that than it might have a person that may have committed adultery multiple times who also wanted to hold a position in the church. In other words, he was identifying me as someone who is a sinner on the same level as someone who has defied the Ten Commandments and therefore unworthy of representing his church.

I cannot believe that God would think my whole life is a sin when my life is mostly the same as anyone else's. I am in a committed and monogamous relationship, I do not cheat on my wife, I go to work, I am a good person for my family and friends—this is not the life of a constant sinner. This is the same life as any other Christian member of a church, but because of one small part of who I am, the church finds me unworthy to represent it. I would need to be a full participant in a church to feel "welcomed and affirmed."

My children needed to feel the same welcoming experience I had as a child, but it was not really available to them as long as I was considered a sinner of this type in the eyes of the church. I have chosen to live an open and non-compartmentalized life, as I believe the other way is fake and lying; that is not who I am today, nor is it healthy for me or my children. It sends a message that my family is less or wrong, and that is not how I feel in the least. I am just as deserving of the same happiness as everyone else and believe my children need to see and live that. Going to church should be an experience and place where you feel the best about who you are and what you can bring to that church community. Knowing that it is okay for you to be there individually, but not okay for you to be really involved, hinders everyone—including the church that chooses not to value the experience or ideas that you may be able to bring to the table.

Being gay and being a Christian sometimes feels like an oxymoron. The church needs to bring its congregation along; not everyone will want to welcome you initially, and that is fine. Not everyone will want you to get married in their church, and that is fine too, but shunning an entire group of people because of who they love is not in the Christian spirit. Jesus would have stood up for the LBGTQ community just as he did for the others that were shunned by society at one time. The change has to start at the top: the pastor, the priest, and the church leaders. They have to stop making this such a divisive subject and start welcoming and affirming all people into their churches. Our world is a very diverse place, but our churches do not seem to want to accept that in a lot of cases. I feel bad for the broader church community and what they may be missing out on, along with the families that long to be included in a church family. It is not easy to find one that will accept a family that may look different but faces the same if not more challenges as every other family. I guess the one thing I would say to the broader church community is: I am sad for you, not me. I have found acceptance for me and my family in one of God's houses. Regardless of whether you want to make me feel welcomed and affirmed, I know I am a good person and on judgment day, only God will be there—it is not your place.

CHAPTER FIVE

THE TRADITIONAL POSITION

WE HAVE CONSIDERED THUS far the arguments in support of the Affirming viewpoint. Now we turn to the Traditionalist viewpoint (the viewpoint I embrace). To be clear, I believe the New Testament affirms sexual relations only between a man and a woman who are committed to each other in marriage, and prohibits *all* sexual intimacy outside of that covenant. In this chapter I will explain why I believe that.

THE BIBLE'S PROHIBITION AGAINST
SAME-SEX SEXUAL BEHAVIOR IS CLEAR

I believe the Bible clearly and unequivocally describes same-sex intimacy as contrary to the design of God. That is the unambiguous message taken from a plain reading of the texts.[1] There is a difference, by the way, between a "plain reading of the text" and "reading the text in isolation." To read a text in isolation is to ignore the related texts that inform and shape our understanding of the text in question. The plain reading of a text is simply the self-evident meaning—an interpretation that does not involve a series of qualifications and maneuverings, conjecture and spin.

Based on the plain reading of the texts, I believe the evidence is compelling: New Testament writers knew about same-sex sexual practices beyond that of abusive, manipulative relationships and, inspired by God's Spirit, censured all same-sex intimacy. The Bible's prohibitions cannot be explained away as mere differences in the kind of sexual behavior we are talking about.

Of course there are those who reach other conclusions based on their belief that we cannot read the texts so simplistically. The most common assertion by those who are Affirming is that the Bible condemns only exploitative forms of same-sex sexual activity. The claim is rooted in the assumption that brutish forms of sexual behavior (such as pederasty) were the only models known to the writers of Scripture. Therefore, the argument goes, of course the Bible condemns same-sex intimacy. The Bible, it is thus assumed, does not address the kind of mutually-fulfilling, committed relationships that are so prominent today.

That assumption, however, is not based on solid evidence. I say that for two basic reasons: (1) It is a big and unverifiable leap to assume the writers of Scripture were unaware of mutually chosen sexual behavior; and (2) should the writers of Scripture have wanted to limit their denunciation to exploitative same-sex sexual practices, they had the means to do so.

Note the following:

- The Bible doesn't say anywhere that it is addressing only crude and ruthless forms of sexual practice.
- The inclusion of lesbian sex in Romans 1:26-27 clearly expands the prohibition beyond man-boy relations (also known as pederasty).
- The Bible speaks of those "inflamed with lust for one another" (Romans 1:26-27), obviously referring to mutually desired and mutually chosen same-sex relationships.

- The Bible denounces both parties in same-sex sex acts (see Leviticus 20:13 and 1 Corinthians 6:9), and would not condemn a victim of sexual abuse.
- There is a Greek word for pederasty (*paiderastia*), and if Paul's writing was limited to that, he could have utilized that word instead of being so broad in his condemnation.

Certainly, the Bible is addressing and condemning abusive sexual relationships. To read the Bible as prohibiting *only* exploitative same-sex activity, however, is an overreach and a denial of the original intent of Scripture.[2]

It is simply inaccurate to assume that consensual, same-sex intimacy among adults was unknown in the biblical world. Matthew Vines (who takes the Affirming position) acknowledges several ancient texts confirming that, in biblical days, bisexual attraction and behaviors were well-known.[3] In *What Does the Bible Really Teach About Homosexuality?* Kevin DeYoung cites and quotes a long list of secular scholars who note the wide range of same-sex sexual practices in the day of the Bible; not just exploitative practices.[4] And N. T. Wright, academic hero of many of us noted this when interviewed on the topic:

> One thing I do know as an ancient historian is that there is nothing in contemporary understanding and experience of homosexual condition and behavior that was unknown in the first century. . . .
>
> Paul will have known the full range of stuff. So the idea that, "Oh, well, in the first century they didn't know what we know now with our scientific knowledge" . . . it's a little bit of Enlightenment arrogance again, actually.[5]

Granted, much of the same-sex sexual behavior in the Bible's day was oppressive and violent and not like the consensual and monogamous gay relationships of today. But not all same-sex sexual behavior in the Bible's day qualified as oppressive and violent. Not all of it was between men and boys. Not all same-sex sexual acts were forced onto unwilling participants.

My own quick scan of the topic of same-sex intimacy in the ancient Greco-Roman world provided several confirmations of the presence of non-exploitative same-sex intimacy, although exploitative relationships such as pederasty are confirmed as, indeed, deplorably common. Same-sex attraction was both well known and well documented. Consider this depiction of same-sex intimacy in ancient Greece from the *Stanford Encyclopedia of Philosophy*:

> Probably the most frequent assumption of sexual orientation is that persons can respond erotically to beauty in either sex. Diogenes Laeurtius, for example, wrote of Alcibiades, the Athenian general and politician of the 5th century B.C., "in his adolescence he drew away the husbands from their wives, and as a young man the wives from their husbands." (Quoted in Greenberg, 1988, 144) Some persons were noted for their exclusive interests in persons of one gender. For example, Alexander the Great and the founder of Stoicism, Zeno of Citium, were known for their exclusive interest in boys and other men. Such persons, however, are generally portrayed as the exception. Furthermore, the issue of what gender one is attracted to is seen as an issue of taste or preference, rather than as a moral issue.[6]

Stanley Grenz rightly contends that to claim no one in the biblical world knew of same-sex marriage "fails to take into consideration the presence of homosexual unions in ancient Greek and Roman culture." Grenz notes that same-sex weddings were not unheard of, and thus posits: "Paul, therefore, was likely aware of the possibility of same-sex marriage."[7]

It seems clear to me: those who penned Scripture knew about same-sex sexual behavior beyond that of pederasty and other exploitative relationships, but did not limit their denunciations to those negative activities. They denounced all same-sex intimacy.

Does anyone seriously believe, Robert Gagnon asked, that if the Corinthian Christians had written back to Paul, explained that in their church were two men in a same-sex intimate relationship but the men were truly in love, that Paul would have responded, "Oh, I'm not talking about them"?[8] I believe the unequivocal answer is "No."

Even in granting the possibility that the Bible is speaking primarily about exploitative same-sex sex, we still have to follow Scripture in the direction that these texts clearly point: same-sex sexual behavior is prohibited. For us to grant permission (despite admirable motives) where the Bible does not grant permission is a grave error.

MALE/FEMALE INTIMACY IS BUILT
INTO THE "NATURAL ORDER"

In Romans 1:26-27 note the use of "natural" and "unnatural."

> Because of this, God gave them over to shameful lusts. Even their women exchanged natural sexual relations for unnatural ones. In the same way the men also abandoned natural relations with women and were inflamed with lust for one another. Men committed shameful acts with other men.

"It's Adam and Eve, not Adam and Steve," some crassly say. While such flippant and simplistic statements are not helpful to the conversation, there is indeed a "natural" order reflected in the creation story that helps undergird the rest of the biblical texts prohibiting same-sex intimacy.

Affirmers might call our attention to the fact that Paul also uses a similar term (*very nature*) to argue against long hair for men (1 Corinthians 11:14). If I am reading the context and flow of 1 Corinthians correctly, however, when addressing the length of men's hair Paul is using this term in the sense of that which is *customary*. The "unnatural" sense of same-sex unions, on the other hand, goes beyond the idea of everyday expectations.

By "natural" the New Testament, in Romans 1:26-27, is referring to the created, intended order—the physical union of people of the opposite sex. In Romans 1, "natural" versus "unnatural" is a theological statement, not a cultural observation. There Paul is assuming the timeless principles of the holiness code ("Don't conform to the moral laxity around you") in Leviticus 18, and alluding to the clear male-female sexuality taught in the first chapter of Genesis.[9]

It is helpful to note that, in Romans 1:26, the word *unnatural* is a translation of the Greek words *para physin*. That phrase, *para physin*, "unnatural," was commonly used in other literature of the day to speak of anomalous sexual behavior, including same-sex sexual intimacy.[10] "Unnatural," meaning contrary to the divine design, was a common description of same-sex intimacy from Plato to Polycarp.[11]

Therefore, based on the use of *unnatural* in other literature of the time, as well as the context and flow of Romans 1:26-27, Paul's intent here is that the "natural" (divinely designed) sexual relationship is male/female. Anything else is a distortion of what God intended for the expression of our sexuality.

John Stott put it like this:

> The reason for the biblical prohibitions (against homosexual behavior in the first century) is the same reason why modern loving homosexual partnerships must also be condemned, namely that they are incompatible with God's created order (heterosexual monogamy). And since that order was established by creation not culture, its validity is both permanent and universal.[12]

It is important to note that the complementary relationships spoken of here have to do with sexuality, not vocational ministry. Our church, for example, took a Traditional position on sexuality but affirms and ordains women in ministry. The position that the natural, created order includes complementary maleness and femaleness does not necessarily imply anything about female roles in the church (or in the home). From my perspective, the discussion about God's intentions for the physical joining of people of the opposite sex and the discussion about whether women should be pastors or should be submissive in marriage are very different.

THE PRIORITY OF BIBLICAL WITNESS

An honest submission to our best understanding of the biblical witness is more important than our experience and reason. As a fan of John Wesley, I find the Wesleyan quadrilateral fascinating. Wesley is credited with the awareness that theological thinking should reflect a balance of four proofs: Scripture, experience, reason, and tradition. I would concur that it is imprudent, even impossible, to interpret God's revelation without the invocation of experience, reason, and tradition.

Yet for Wesley, Scripture was the clear test of the other three, and appropriately so. Neither experience nor reason nor tradition should be considered on the same level of authority as the Bible. The balance is difficult to maintain, and yet it is critical.

It appears to me that the position taken by some people promotes experience and reasoning over the authority of Scripture. The Affirming position, from my viewpoint, elevates the rights and scrutiny of mortals over the revelation of the Creator of the universe.

It is one thing to debate the *interpretation* of Scripture; it is quite another to subject Scripture to human approval. Of course, it would be an unscrupulous overreach for me to imply that everyone who wants churches to approve same-sex intimacy holds the Bible in such disregard. There is enough of that on the part of advocates of same-sex relationships, however, that the Affirming argument is weakened.

I do not doubt the sincerity of my Christian brothers and sisters who advocate for the legitimization of same-sex intimacy or marriage. I believe most of them are motivated by compassion. However, I do not believe my Christian friends can appeal to biblical authority to support their position.

Those who are Affirming can appeal to admirable motives, such as kindness, fairness, and inclusion. Yet I believe that they cannot bolster their posture with biblical exegesis. In fact, I believe those who Affirm have to attempt somehow to explain away the plain reading of Scripture that limits the beautiful gift of sexual intimacy to the covenant of marriage between a man and a woman.

I further believe Affirming viewpoints expressed by words such as "our stories become the medium of God's very revelation"[13] are so subjective as to be dangerous. While God's grace and mercy are certainly seen in our stories, to use human stories as the determiners of divine principles is rather presumptuous.

THE WRONG SIDE OF HISTORY IS NOT SO BAD

None of us wants to be judged by future generations as ignorant. Even if people of the future concede, "They were products of their time," that's still not flattering. In other words, no one wants to be on the wrong side of history.

It is often said that I and others who hold the Traditional position are just that—on the wrong side of history. That phrase, "on the wrong side of history," is, of course, intended to shame people like me into a more enlightened, progressive stance on the topic. The phrase communicates that Traditionalists are simply slow to catch on, and that eventually people will look back on those holding such views as old-school and, at best, ignorant.

Even Matthew Vines, whose tone I generally appreciate, resorted to this tactic when contending for an Affirming position: "For the first sixteen hundred years of church history every major Christian leader and theologian believed that the earth stood at the center of the universe."[14] The simplistic implication is that the unwillingness to bless same-sex sexuality is tantamount to a declaration that the sun revolves around the earth.

John Shore compares those of us who are not supportive of same-sex intimacy to the Japanese soldiers stranded in the jungles of the Philippines who continued to wage guerrilla warfare even after WWII had ended. He goes on to say:

> The bottom line on the whole LGBT-Christianity issue is that within what historically is an astonishingly short period of time (yay Internet!), we have reached Ye Olde

Tipping Point. And from this point on that seesaw will only continue tipping further to the left. That certainly works for me personally. For verily am I just ever so slightly weary of hollering into the jungle for the deeply confused, bizarrely obdurate Christian combatants in there to stop fighting.[15]

It's hard to take Shore seriously when he makes comments like that, but I believe he is right to say that culture is moving rapidly toward the widespread affirmation of same-sex intimacy. I do believe it is very possible that same-sex intimacy will be accepted by the majority of Christians within the next few decades. The trend seems clear.

A trend does not invalidate, however, an understanding of sacred Scripture that limits sex to the covenant marriage between a man and a woman. Right and wrong are not determined by majority opinion or trends but by divine revelation.

While the trend may be undeniable, I don't believe the widespread affirmation of same-sex relationships will be a good thing. The free love of the 1960s, for example, changed attitudes in our culture about sex outside marriage. The birth control pill made sex without fear of pregnancy a reality and fueled the changing attitudes about sexual intimacy. And I don't think the sexual revolution was a positive development. Look at the curse of pornography, the rise in sexually transmitted diseases, the number of unwanted pregnancies and abortions, and the broken lives and hearts resulting from promiscuity.

Moreover, perhaps the wrong side of history argument is not a foregone conclusion! Maybe the trend is not so inevitable. As an example, one would have thought the Roe versus Wade decision in 1973 would have settled the debate over abortion for Americans. Yet the debate continues, and there are indications of a swing in public opinion back toward a more traditional position.

Bottom line, I'm willing to live with the charge that I am on the wrong side of history. It is not a bad thing to be on the wrong side of history if history is on the wrong side of morality.

LONGSTANDING TEACHINGS AND BURDEN OF PROOF

The church has been consistent on this subject for two millennia, and thus the burden of proof for the overturning of church teaching lies with the advocates of same-sex intimacy. Advocates of same-sex relationships and marriage fail to make a case sufficient to overturn the longstanding teaching of the church. The departure by mainline denominations and some evangelicals from the conventional, orthodox church teaching on sexuality is *despite* the evidence not *in light of* the evidence.

And let's not understate the fact that the blessing of same-sex intimate relationships is indeed a redefinition of, arguably, the most important human relationship: marriage. The blessing of same-sex intimate relationships is even a reframing of what it is to be human, for our maleness and femaleness are rooted in creation. It is a serious matter—this attempt to redefine sexuality. If one wants to do so, one has to look somewhere other than the Bible.

KEY WEAKNESSES OF THE AFFIRMING POSITION

I believe preconceived ideas shape Affirming biblical interpretation. It is my opinion that many who advocate for same-sex relationships have reached their conclusions either (1) before doing the serious work of biblical interpretation or (2) after ignoring the serious work of biblical interpretation.

Relationships with gay persons, feelings that the church is being unfair and judgmental, convictions that a God of love would not limit the joy of gay persons by prohibiting their loving relationships, and so on, have prompted people to look for loopholes. It seems to me that many have "imposed a wishful interpretation on the biblical passages."[16]

Those who are Affirming seem to begin with the assumption, for example, that because God is loving, he would not create someone with a gay orientation and then deny him or her the option of the personal fulfillment that comes through a lifelong, loving relationship. Then they re-read the texts dealing with same-sex intimacy through those lenses, seeking support for their already-arrived-at position. Those who advocate for the legitimacy of same-sex intimacy approach the Scriptures with a presupposition.

Love, powerful force that it is, has compelled lots of good people to change their minds. Often that love is directed toward a family member who has come out. Often that love is directed toward the throngs of people pushed to the margins. Love, of course, always is admirable. I simply believe that heartfelt sympathy has trumped straightforward biblical interpretation for many.

It is difficult to discover the meaning of a text if we already have an assumption about the "correct" interpretation. Looking to the Bible to justify one's predetermined position is not new, but neither is it right.

The following by Mark Achtemeier is one of many examples of the "presume, then interpret" approach of which I'm speaking: "I knew that in order to fully embrace the hopeful conclusions I had turned up about God's blessing of same-sex relationships, I would need to find a way to positively incorporate these traditional fragments into the big picture of the Bible's witness."[17]

Note that Achtemeier arrived at his "hopeful conclusions about God's blessing of same-sex relationships" and *then* found a way to "positively incorporate these traditional fragments into the big picture of the Bible's witness."

Here is another insightful quote from Achtemeier:

> I realized it was not enough simply to recognize that traditional condemnations of homosexuality were mistaken. Such a recognition wouldn't carry much credibility unless it was accompanied by a truer, better reading of the Bible that showed in a positive way how gay people were recipients of God's blessing. It was to the task of developing that truer, better reading that I now had to turn.[18]

I don't mean to imply that Achtemeier is intentionally manipulative. I don't know him, and certainly do not intend to impugn his motives. It does appear to me, however, that Achtemeier (like so many) reached a conclusion and then looked for biblical justification for his conclusion so as to appeal to his more traditional brothers and sisters.

Admittedly, none of us can completely bracket out our assumptions. But prejudgment surely minimizes the possibility of sound interpretation. And in both my readings and personal conversations with those who Affirm, it seems to be a common practice among them to seek biblical evidence for a decision at which they have already arrived.

In all fairness, it is not only advocates of same-sex intimacy who are guilty of this. That kind of biblical interpretation is all too common. Nevertheless, the preconceptions that I perceive on the part of so many who are Affirming cast serious doubt on their use of the Bible to justify same-sex relationships.

Of course, scores of people affirm both the legitimacy of same-sex intimacy and the authority of Scripture. I believe it is possible to enthusiastically acknowledge the Bible's clout and yet read it with a bias that clouds its intended meaning. There is enough wiggle room within such a phrase as "a high view of Scripture" that even a claim that we believe in the Bible's authority does not guarantee acceptance of, and submission to, its message.

The church's loss of people over this certainly is heartbreaking. However (and I'm not trying to sound pious), we cannot abdicate our responsibility to the revelation of God as we understand it. One of the arguments for an Affirming stance is that evangelicals are seen as judgmental, pharisaical, and closed-minded. Thus, the reasoning goes, we are losing lots of people who are choosing to distance themselves from the church.

On the one hand, these losses are indeed heartbreaking. To have anyone despise or distrust the church is disastrous. It is true that our words and tones have not only turned people off to church; there have been those who have either left the Christian faith altogether or chosen not to consider the Christian faith at all. We must not fail to appreciate how tragic that is. Ken Wilson is right: "Causing an unnecessary disincentive to follow Christ is a serious offense, at least as serious as failing to uphold a moral good."[19]

On the other hand, it would be unwise to reach moral conclusions based on how others will react to us. Jesus recognized that. Remember the following from John 6:53-67:

> Jesus said to them, "Very truly I tell you, unless you eat the flesh of the Son of Man and drink his blood, you have no life in you." . . . On hearing it, many of his disciples said, "This is a hard teaching. Who can accept it?" Aware that his disciples were grumbling about this, Jesus said

to them, "Does this offend you?" . . . From this time many of his disciples turned back and no longer followed him. "You do not want to leave too, do you?" Jesus asked the Twelve.

It would be neither faithful nor honest to relax one's position on same-sex intimacy just so that one's church will grow numerically. It would be disingenuous for a Traditionalist like me to pretend I don't believe same-sex intimacy is wrong, even if the motivation is as wonderful as reaching young adults.

Moreover, the idea that if the church were on the Affirming side of this debate we could attract more people to us is naïve. Even if all of us were to declare we are completely open to same-sex intimacy and embrace same-sex marriage, we would certainly be demonized for other things. Consider, for example, these hard truths.

- The claim that Jesus is the only way to God is deemed narrow-minded.
- Our insistence that people (straight people included) not have sex until they are married is thought to be antiquated.
- Hell is thought to be a ghoulish fantasy.
- The teaching that people without Jesus are "lost" and need to be "saved" is taken by many as an offense.
- The cross has been considered a "stumbling block" and "foolishness" for two millennia (1 Corinthians 1:23).

Thus, while I appreciate the desire not to be thought of as archaic, puritanical, and pharisaical, it is surprisingly gullible to think we will be embraced by our surrounding society if we merely declare ourselves to be so open-minded that we now affirm same-sex sexual behavior.

Same-sex relationships and divorce are, in fact, different. It is perhaps true that the church has become too soft on divorce and remarriage. I would not want to try to defend any willingness to condone, wink at, turn a blind eye to, or overlook the destructive impact of divorce in the church. However, Robert Gagnon makes a terribly important point here:

> For the situation (of a divorced person) to be comparable to a self-affirming, practicing homosexual, a person would have to be engaged in self-avowed serial divorce actions. . . . Some people are divorced against their will or initiate divorce for justifiable cause against a philandering or violent spouse. Such people should be distinguished from those who divorce a spouse in order to have love affairs with others or to achieve "self-fulfillment."[20]

The number of divorces and the resulting brokenness among Jesus-followers is regrettable. Divorce itself, however, is not comparable to an ongoing same-sex relationship or marriage. As I see it, divorce is an event—often a sinful event—but not a way of life. I find broad (though not unanimous) agreement among Christians that there is indeed a distinction between the failure of a marriage and the choice to live in an ongoing intimate relationship with someone of the same sex. As I see it, divorce is a tragic, and often sinful, occurrence; gay marriage (or an ongoing same-sex relationship) is a life choice that places one in enduring rebellion against the design of our Creator.

However, I would not disagree that we should be more discerning when appointing to leadership those who are divorced. The circumstances surrounding the divorces and how people have lived after those divorces should be factors when we are considering divorced people for leadership. That would certainly be consistent with what I believe to be higher qualifications for spiritual leadership.

Perhaps the large number of divorces in the church and the desire not to exclude people has resulted in less stringent criteria than we are applying to same-sex relationships. If this conversation about leadership and sexuality were to result in a more biblically-balanced approach to leadership and divorce, then I see that as a helpful thing.

The slavery error does not justify advocacy of same-sex intimacy. Slavery and its justification by Christians is a tragic chapter in the history of southern churches. Yet, the logic of so many Affirmers ("We misinterpreted Scripture regarding slavery, therefore we must be misinterpreting Scripture regarding same-sex intimacy") is unconvincing. Everyone I know acknowledges the tragic sins of slavery, but our deep regret over those sins does not justify a re-reading of Scripture on LGBT issues. Nor does a re-reading on same-sex intimacy somehow atone for our sins regarding slavery.

Some African Americans, in fact, resent the co-opting of the imagery and principles of the Civil Rights Movement by those calling for the affirmation of same-sex sexual intimacy.[21]

The fact that only a small number of biblical texts address same-sex intimacy and that Jesus is silent on the topic are not arguments for same-sex intimacy. The contention that the church should not speak against same-sex intimacy because the Bible only speaks to the subject a few times, and because there is no record of Jesus mentioning it, is unpersuasive. An argument from silence is, in fact, a tenuous argument.

I would counter that the Bible doesn't talk about it much for the same reason that I didn't talk about it much for the first two decades of my ministry: it wasn't such a big issue. In the context from which the Bible emerged, same-sex sexual behavior was assumed to be wrong. Neither Jesus nor the writers of the New Testament would have felt the need to argue a position that was so widely held.

It is quite a stretch to assume Jesus would have had a different position than the Hebrew Scriptures.[22] In fact, when Jesus did speak to such topics as marriage, he reflected a firm interpretation of the sexual morality of the Jewish Law (for example, lusting is the same as committing adultery, from Matthew 5:28). Regarding sexuality, Jesus strictly advocated for the covenant love between a man and a woman (Matthew 19:4-6; Mark 10:5-9).

We could make the same point about Paul. For Paul to spend a lot of time arguing against same-sex intimacy would have been overkill. Most in Paul's audience would have taken for granted that God's intention for sexual intimacy is for married men and women.

An appeal to love is no justification for immorality. Walter Wink is one who has said that love is the overriding biblical sex ethic, and that love negates and overrides the isolated restrictions on same-sex intimacy. The following is from Wink's article in *Christian Century*. I include it here because it demonstrates, in my view, the weakness of the so-called love argument:

> The crux of the matter, it seems to me, is simply that the Bible has no sexual ethic. There is no biblical sex ethic. The Bible knows only a love ethic, which is constantly being brought to bear on whatever sexual mores are dominant in any given country, or culture, or period.[23]

The impotence of Wink's argument should be obvious to anyone who believes in the authority of Scripture. In fact,

Wink's anthropocentric logic reminds me of the lines from an old pop song: "It can't be wrong when it feels so right."

John Stott understood the appeal to love as a justification for same-sex intimacy and appropriately warned against it: "Quality of love is not the only yardstick by which to measure what is good or right."[24] Love between two people, no matter how sincere, does not validate an invalid, self-serving interpretation of revealed truth through Scripture.

We humans have an uncanny ability to rationalize. Since the fall (humankind's first sin and its catastrophic impact) humans have been born with a sin nature, the overwhelming tendency to do the wrong thing. With the fall came also the curse of an ability to rationalize or explain away our sinful choices.

Are people attempting to alleviate their cognitive dissonance—the mental and spiritual discomfort we experience when we hold contradictory beliefs or values? That could be what is behind the re-interpretation of Scripture and the aggressive efforts by some to mainstream same-sex intimacy in our society.

There is an alarming dismissal of non-Western voices. Lots of our Christian friends around the world are surprised and disappointed by the Affirming positions taken by so many Christians in the West. And, quite frankly, the perspectives on this topic offered by Christians in the Majority World have been written off by lots of Western Christians. I have heard Affirming Christians from the West arrogantly belittle the worldview of Traditional-minded Christians from around the world. That is disappointing.

If I am right, and the authority for what we believe and practice should be Scripture rightly interpreted, then of course we must examine the Scripture. Exegesis is fundamental to our discussion, and it is to exegesis that we turn to in the next chapter.

TESTIMONIAL

FROM A SINGLE, GAY CHRISTIAN
GREGORY COLES

I'll never forget the first time I was turned away from a ministry opportunity because I was gay.

It wasn't because I was gay and sexually active, or pursuing future sexual activity. I'm committed to following the Jesus revealed in the Bible, and as I understand him, same-sex sexual expression is something I'm called to abstain from. To be frank, I've never actually had sex. (I've repented from plenty of other sins, but that hardly makes me an anomaly among Christians of any orientation.)

I was turned away because I was gay. Just that. Just the state of being persistently attracted to the same sex and being honest about my experience with the people around me was enough to disqualify me from that ministry.

Stories like this one—and much worse—aren't rare. Last week, a celibate, gay, Christian friend of mine was removed from his position as a counselor at a Christian camp because of concerns that parents wouldn't want him around their children. Another friend was hired by a church and then fired less than a month later after congregants complained and gossiped about his sexuality. I've known teachers who lost classrooms, speakers who lost platforms, and volunteers who lost invitations to serve.

It's not about our sexual activity. It's not about our theology of sexual ethics.

It's about being gay.

Sometimes the reasoning is pragmatic. "*We* don't have a problem with you," say the people who turn us away. "But we don't want to risk losing members, worrying parents, or upsetting donors. There's so much good ministry happening, and we don't want your sexual orientation to be a distraction from the Lord's work."

Sometimes people's objections are terminological: "Don't call yourself *gay*. You're *same-sex attracted*. And before you can serve this church body, it's crucial for you to agree with us about the nuances of certain words and the function of language in society."

Sometimes people insist that God wants to turn us straight—that our gay orientation proves the paucity of our prayers, the flaws of our parents, and the ineptitude of our mentors. "The moment you stop praying to be straight," they say, "you've given up on Jesus. To be gay is to be an extra-awful brand of broken."

I don't hold any ill will toward the people who believe these things—or at least, I don't mean to. I know what it's like to believe that gay people should pray themselves into heterosexuality, that the word *gay* is inherently evil, that the honest story of a celibate gay person would be a detriment to the gospel. I used to believe all these things about myself.

But a church where attitudes like these prevail will never be a church where someone like me can fully belong. There's not much use claiming to be a welcoming church for LGBTQ folks if your church considers us all, even the celibate ones, to be a liability; if our orientation is too much of a distraction for us to serve your local church body; if you wish we were tempted toward nice, "normal," straight sexual sins because the temptations we're choosing to say no to gross you out.

If your church wishes that I had just stayed in the closet, gritting my teeth as the years passed in silent loneliness, I'm not really welcome there. I never was. My effigy was welcome, my straight alter ego was welcome, but not *me*.

Today I'm at a wonderful church where I've been really, truly, gloriously welcomed. It's the kind of place that leaves room for honest doubt and sincere disagreement without departing from biblical conviction. I lead worship on Sundays and work with college students during the week and occasionally help with a sports camp for hordes of children in the summer.

I came out to the senior pastor of my church three years ago, and to most of the congregation one year ago. In all the best ways, nothing has changed. I still lead worship. I still work with college students. I still helped with the sports camp last summer, even though I got shingles on my neck and had to cover them with a bandage that made me look like a car accident survivor.

My church's pastoral staff and elder team have committed to standing with me in my journey as a celibate gay Christian. They might not all agree with me about every little nuance of the sexuality conversation—Lord knows I'm fallible—but they believe in the value of making space for me to learn and grow and serve and lead. My sexuality interests them less than my pursuit of Jesus. Instead of trying to remake me in their own image, they faithfully point me to the God who remakes me, bit by bit, in his image.

Both from the pulpit and on the ground, my church honors the vocation of singleness and urges against the idolatry of the nuclear family. When people raise eyebrows at me and wonder whether I ought to belong in the body of Christ, this church body draws me in closer. When a family left our church to protest my leadership in worship as a celibate gay person, no church leader proposed that I ought to step away from the piano for a while instead.

In this church, people don't call me a distraction. They call me a blessing. They open their homes to me and miss me when I'm out of town and hope aloud that I'll stay forever.

Chances are good that I'll have to change jobs—and move to a new city—in a year or two. I hate the thought of losing this church and trying to find another place where I'll be welcomed. I hate the thought of walking through another set of church doors without knowing whether I'll belong, without knowing whether the churches that claim the label "welcoming" will really welcome me.

Still, I believe with all my heart that welcoming churches can and do exist. I pray we find them. I pray we become them.

CHAPTER SIX

WHAT DOES THE BIBLE SAY?

WITH MY PERSONAL OBSERVATIONS, explanations, and declarations out of the way, let's turn to the much more important matter: What does the Bible say? We will cover here the passages most commonly referred to in discussions about same-sex relationships.

GENESIS 1–2

Genesis 1:27 reads, "Male and female he created them." It is not insignificant that in the very beginning males and females are distinct from each other, drawn to each other, find unique companionship in each other, and complement each other. That intrinsic, complementary quality of the male-female relationship is one of the truths underlying the New Testament's prohibitions against same-sex intimacy. The male-female relationship is the divine design.

The first two chapters of Genesis provide an important foundation on which the key New Testament texts build. The weighty and far-reaching words of Jesus himself regarding marriage, found in Matthew 19, are rooted in those two chapters.

"Haven't you read," he replied, "that at the beginning the Creator 'made them male and female,' and said, 'For this reason a man will leave his father and mother and be united to his wife, and the two will become one flesh'? So they are no longer two, but one flesh. Therefore what God has joined together, let no one separate." (Matthew 19:4-6)

ROMANS 1:18-32

The wrath of God is being revealed from heaven against all the godlessness and wickedness of people, who suppress the truth by their wickedness, since what may be known about God is plain to them, because God has made it plain to them. For since the creation of the world God's invisible qualities—his eternal power and divine nature—have been clearly seen, being understood from what has been made, so that people are without excuse.

For although they knew God, they neither glorified him as God nor gave thanks to him, but their thinking became futile and their foolish hearts were darkened. Although they claimed to be wise, they became fools and exchanged the glory of the immortal God for images made to look like a mortal human being and birds and animals and reptiles.

Therefore God gave them over in the sinful desires of their hearts to sexual impurity for the degrading of their bodies with one another. They exchanged the truth about God for a lie, and worshiped and served created things rather than the Creator—who is forever praised. Amen.

Because of this, God gave them over to shameful lusts. Even their women exchanged natural sexual relations for unnatural ones. In the same way the men also abandoned natural relations with women and were inflamed with lust for one another. Men committed shameful acts with other men, and received in themselves the due penalty for their error.

Furthermore, just as they did not think it worthwhile to retain the knowledge of God, so God gave them over to a depraved mind, so that they do what ought not to be done. They have become filled with every kind of wickedness, evil, greed and depravity. They are full of envy, murder, strife, deceit and malice. They are gossips, slanderers, God-haters, insolent, arrogant and boastful; they invent ways of doing evil; they disobey their parents; they have no understanding, no fidelity, no love, no mercy. Although they know God's righteous decree that those who do such things deserve death, they not only continue to do these very things but also approve of those who practice them.

In this text, same-sex sexual behavior is "unnatural," meaning it violates the divine design. The recurring prohibition of same-sex intimacy in Scripture, based on "natural order," is rooted in the language of the creation story. The male-female relationship is "natural" in the most fundamental meaning of that word.

The people addressed here are attracted to each other; therefore Romans 1 challenges the argument that the same-sex sexual relationships addressed in the Bible are only abusive, exploitative relationships. Don't overlook the importance of this. Earlier I noted the popular Affirming argument that the Bible's prohibitions are not against monogamous, committed gay relationships. Rather, many contend, the Bible is condemning those who would force themselves sexually onto people of the same sex. Pederasty and the trafficking of people for same-sex sex acts, it is said, are the evils that the Bible rails against, not loving relationships.

But Romans 1 speaks of mutual attraction, even describing people who are "inflamed with lust for one another" (v. 27).

This is a description of people who want to be together; there is nothing forced about the same-sex intimacy described here. Thus we can be clear that New Testament writers (1) knew about mutually chosen sexual behavior, and (2) did not exclude consensual acts from their denunciation of same-sex sexual behavior. To read the Bible as prohibiting only abusive, exploitative same-sex activity, one has to ignore Romans 1.[1]

The inclusion of lesbian sex here bolsters the argument that the Bible denounces all same-sex intimacy. There are not many references to female same-sex sexual behavior or relationships in ancient writings, but the inclusion of women in this text reminds us that the Bible is not merely addressing such evils as male temple prostitutes or men having sex with boys.

In Romans 1, same-sex sexual behavior is presented as a reflection of an overall idolatrous mindset. The most sobering insight I find in Romans 1 is how God inspires Paul to link illicit sexual behavior to idolatry: "They exchanged the truth about God for a lie, and worshiped and served created things rather than the Creator" (v. 25).

Same-sex sexual behavior is offered here as an example (among many, of course) of our egocentric idolization of something very different from God's intent. It is idolatrous in that it results from an elevation of one's pleasure or opinion over the loving intent of our Creator. Romans 1 condemns the willingness to prioritize human ideas about sexuality over the self-revelation of God.

If one's idea about sexuality takes priority over God's plan for our sexuality, that is idolatry. I believe that "when human beings engage in homosexual activity, they enact an outward and visible sign of an inward and spiritual reality: the rejection of the Creator's design."[2] The same can be said, of course, about any sexual intimacy outside of the marriage of a man and a woman.

Romans 1 has a warning for those who advocate for same-sex sexual behavior. In the final phrase from this first chapter of Romans, Paul writes to those who "do these very things," but does not stop there. He also writes to those who "also approve of those who practice them" (v. 32). Certainly the Bible is speaking here to those who endorse inappropriate behavior. That warning should not be lost in this debate. Yes, I know how prudish it sounds, but I believe the Bible tells us here that giving approval to same-sex sexual behavior, no matter how loving our motives, is not healthy for the church and not healthy for a society.

Should we advocate for everyone's rights and respect people with varying viewpoints? Certainly. Should we fight bullying and distance ourselves from those in the Christian family who make indefensible comments such as blaming natural disasters on people who are gay? Of course. But our current trend toward the endorsement of any sexual intimacy outside of the marriage of a man and a women, and the aggressive vilification of those with traditional values, cannot be healthy.

Note this commentary on Romans 1:32 from Paul J. Achthemeier:

> It may strike us odd that Paul (v. 32) seems to think approving such acts is worse than doing them, but what he is pointing to is the fact that those who do such things not only do them in their own lives but make them a matter of public encouragement for others to follow. . . . Such people, Paul says, seek to make the measure of their sinful conduct the norm for the conduct of others. It is the desire to make private sin the measure of public conduct that Paul is condemning here.[3]

Not long ago in the Western world, we were debating such things as whether gay and lesbian partners should be granted family visitation for their dying partners in hospitals. Lots of Traditionalists answered "Yes!" and in many ways advocated for the rights of gay and lesbian couples. Now those same Traditionalists are often called bigoted and worse because we will not affirm same-sex sexual behavior.

Within a shockingly short few years the requests for acceptance have turned into demands for affirmation. That attempt by many to redefine tolerance is why so many complain of a "gay agenda."

A set-up? Many on the Affirming side would caution that we not read too much into this text. They ask, "Was Paul really condemning same-sex sexual behavior, or was he merely using something he knew would get his audience riled up in order to point out their hypocrisy?" In other words, was he just setting them up?

In Romans 1:18-32, Paul indeed lists acts that would have been abhorrent to the Jewish Christians. Among those abhorrent acts is same-sex sexual behavior such as women exchanging "natural sexual relations for unnatural ones" and men committing "shameful acts with other men."

We can imagine his Jewish-background audience taking the bait. We can picture them hearing Paul's list of exploits they would have found so repulsive and in return crying, "Amen! Preach, brother! Those folks are awful."

But Paul sets the hook when he turns the mirror on his audience in Romans 2:1! He challenges them:

> You, therefore, have no excuse, you who pass judgment on someone else, for at whatever point you judge another, you are condemning yourself, because you who pass judgment do the same things.

Yes, Paul does set them up and proclaim that their judgmental hypocrisy is every bit as wrong as these things they rail against. It was a stroke of communication genius.

His tactic does not, however, mean that the list of attitudes and behaviors with which Paul set them up are acceptable! Paul does not negate the wrongfulness of same sex sexual practice any more that he negates the wrongfulness of the other sins listed here, including envy, murder, strife, and deceit.

It's as if a pastor today were to declare to certain congregations: "Same-sex intimacy violates our Creator's intentions! Same-sex intimacy falls short of God's plans! And sins like that disgust you, right?"

"You got it, Pastor!" the crowd might exclaim self-righteously. "Preach on!"

Now the skillful preacher has them where he wants them, and he sets the hook . . .

"Well, get off your high horses!" the pastor proclaims, stunning the crowd. "Those of you who decry the gay agenda should be careful. Some of you are equally guilty—guilty of greed, gossip, pride, and bigotry. Careful, friends—your condescension and hypocrisy are showing!"

If a pastor were to do this, the pastor would be exposing the congregation's duplicity, just as Paul did. But the pastor's ploy to expose the listeners' hypocrisy does not condone same-sex sexual behavior any more than Paul did in Romans 1.

1 CORINTHIANS 6:9-10

Or do you not know that wrongdoers will not inherit the kingdom of God? Do not be deceived: Neither the sexually immoral nor idolaters nor adulterers nor men who have sex with men nor thieves nor the greedy nor drunkards nor slanderers nor swindlers will inherit the kingdom of God.

In this New International Version translation, the phrase "men who have sex with men" translates two Greek words, *malakoi* and *arsenokoitai*. *Malakoi* literally means "soft ones." Bauer's *Greek-English Lexicon of the New Testament and Other Early Christian Literature* translates *malakoi* as "soft, effeminate" in regard to people.

Arsenokoitai is a rare, compound word (maybe even a word of Paul's invention)—conjoining "man" and "bed"—leading to the possible literal translation as "man-bedders" or "men who take men to bed." In Bauer's, the word *arsenokoitai* is simply translated "a male who engages in sexual activity with a person of his own sex, *pederast*."

The New American Standard version tends to be a bit more literal than many other translations. Note that the NASB translates those two Greek words separately instead of in one phrase as the NIV does:

> Or do you not know that the unrighteous will not inherit the kingdom of God? Do not be deceived; neither fornicators, nor idolaters, nor adulterers, nor effeminate [*malakoi*], nor homosexuals [*arsenokoitai*], nor thieves, nor the covetous, nor drunkards, nor revilers, nor swindlers, will inherit the kingdom of God.

The Anchor Bible (Doubleday, 1976) is another translation that separates *malakoi* and *arsenokoitai* in 1 Corinthians 6:9:

> Stop deceiving yourselves. Neither sexually immoral persons, idolaters, adulterers, effeminate men, male homosexuals, thieves, greedy people, drunkards, revilers, nor swindlers will inherit God's kingdom.

These two words (*malakoi* and *arsenokotai*) are key to the present debate over same-sex sexual behavior. Those who support and advocate for monogamous same-sex relationships often contend that this combination of *malakoi* and *arsenokoitai* in 1 Corinthians 6:9-10 indicates the relationship of men and boys known as pederasty or perhaps male prostitution. They say that "soft ones" indicates the forced participant in the sex act. So Affirmers contend that this is not talking about two people who are in a consensual, monogamous, marriage relationship.[4]

I simply do not find that interpretation compelling. It is much more likely that *malakoi* refers to the consenting though more passive partner in a gay sexual relationship, while *arsenokoitai* refers to the more assertive partner in the relationship. To be explicit, this is probably a reference to the one penetrated (*malakoi*) and the one penetrating (*arsenokoitai*). Even a number of Affirming scholars admit to this interpretation.[5] That is why the NIV combines those two words into the translation, "men who have sex with men."

It seems clear to me that it would have been simple and easy if Paul had intended to speak of exploitative sexual behavior. To retranslate these texts, giving the texts such radically different meanings than a plain reading indicates, is rather presumptuous and appears to be an attempt to justify conclusions already reached.

So, here is a really big question: Can sexually active gay people be true Christians? Some read 1 Corinthians 6:9-10 and conclude that they cannot. There is, in fact, a solemn warning that the people listed there, including "men who have sex with men" but also including "thieves, greedy, drunkards," and more, "will not inherit the kingdom of God."

A similar message is found in Ephesians 5:3-5:

But among you there must not be even a hint of sexual immorality, or of any kind of impurity, or of greed, because these are improper for God's holy people. Nor should there be obscenity, foolish talk or coarse joking, which are out of place, but rather thanksgiving. For of this you can be sure: No immoral, impure or greedy person—such a person is an idolater—has any inheritance in the kingdom of Christ and of God.

Frankly, these two texts are difficult to interpret. Of one thing we can be sure: they cover many more people than just gay men and women. Our discussion should be about whether any of the people on this list will inherit the kingdom of God, and not many of us are exempt from the charges found here! Most of us are at times greedy or have impure thoughts (or actions). How many of us have been guilty of idolatry—letting something in our lives rise in importance above God? And since "foolish talk" is included in this list, lots of us are in trouble!

It seems to me that these warnings in 1 Corinthians 6 and Ephesians 5 belong in the "It is easier for a camel to go through the eye of a needle than for someone who is rich to enter the kingdom of God" (Matthew 19:24) category. All these verses demonstrate the depravity of humanity and the desperate need for grace that all of us share.

What is absolutely clear is that the discussion of these two verses from 1 Corinthians 6 and Ephesians 5 is far broader than same-sex intimacy. If these texts say sexually immoral people cannot enter the kingdom, then they likewise say lots of others are going to end up on the outside looking in. We simply have to trust this puzzling matter to our merciful, just God.

1 TIMOTHY 1:8-11

We know that the law is good if one uses it properly. We also know that the law is made not for the righteous but for lawbreakers and rebels, the ungodly and sinful, the unholy and irreligious, for those who kill their fathers or mothers, for murderers, for the sexually immoral, for those practicing homosexuality, for slave traders and liars and perjurers—and for whatever else is contrary to the sound doctrine that conforms to the gospel concerning the glory of the blessed God, which he entrusted to me.

The word translated as "for those practicing homosexuality" in 1 Timothy 1:10 is *arsenokoitai*. Its placement in the sentence, and whether its placement is important, is the topic of much conversation.

Those who affirm same-sex relationships often note that the phrase "those practicing homosexuality" is placed between the phrases "the sexually immoral" and "slave traders." They contend that the order in which Paul placed these words indicates Paul is talking about the sex trafficking of boys, not the mutually consenting and fulfilling gay relationships we know today.

There are indeed various ways of viewing the unusual word *arsenokoitai*. So it is certainly possible that 1 Timothy 1:10 references something other than what we know today as consensual same-sex intimacy. To make that assumption, however, is a stretch—a stretch not supported by the majority of biblical scholars.

When we consider the use of *arsenokoitai* in 1 Corinthians 6, any argument that *arsenokoitai* in 1 Timothy 1 does not refer to same-sex intimacy has to be viewed as weak. Because same-sex intimacy was common in Ephesus,[6] where Timothy was serving, the plain reading of 1 Timothy 1:10 is that God inspired Paul simply to write about same-sex sexual practice, including consensual sex.

John R. W. Stott wrote that *arsenokoitēs* here means "practising male homosexuals."[7] Gordon Fee contended that the word refers to "male coital homosexuality."[8] These two highly regarded students of Scripture, Stott and Fee, have the weight of evidence on their sides.

LEVITICUS 18:22; 20:13

> Do not have sexual relations with a man as one does with a woman; that is detestable. . . .
>
> If a man has sexual relations with a man as one does with a woman, both of them have done what is detestable. They are to be put to death; their blood will be on their own heads.

Leviticus does not offer the last or best word on our topic. In fact, advocates of committed same-sex relationships often point to the many practices and restrictions promoted in the book of Leviticus that Christians no longer observe, thus questioning why Traditionalists would use anything at all from Leviticus to support the Traditional position.

There are certainly ceremonial and dietary regulations in Leviticus that are not re-affirmed in the New Testament. Yet this section of Leviticus provides important background for New Testament morality.

These passages from Leviticus fall within the holiness code (chapters 17–26), which set the nation of Israel apart from their pagan neighbors. Leviticus 18:3-4 describes the purpose of this holiness code:

> You must not do as they do in Egypt, where you used to live, and you must not do as they do in the land of Canaan, where I am bringing you. Do not follow their practices. You must obey my laws and be careful to follow my decrees. I am the LORD your God.

This concern for holiness is certainly a priority in the New Testament as well. There are, in fact, enough commonalities between Leviticus and Paul's writings that the apostle appears to have been thinking about this ancient passage of Scripture, together with the design of male and female relationships in the creation story, as he wrote about sexuality. So, while a Traditionalist argument based largely on Leviticus is unconvincing, ignoring Leviticus altogether is unwarranted and unwise. These are broadly applicable instructions on morality, not just situational guidelines for ceremonies which Christians no longer practice.

GENESIS 19:1-29

Genesis 19 tells the story of Sodom and Gomorrah, which includes the request in verse 5 that Lot send out his male guests for their sexual pleasure:

> They called to Lot, "Where are the men who came to you tonight? Bring them out to us so that we can have sex with them."

It is difficult to build a case about monogamous, committed same-sex relationships around this passage. It is true that the negative assessment of same-sex relationships is reflected in the commentary on Genesis 19 found in 2 Peter 2:6-10 and Jude 7. Yet the issue in Genesis 19 is violent sexual behavior, attempted gang rape, if you will. The main point of this text is not the prohibition of committed gay relationships, so this text is not much help to us in our present debate.

JUDE 7

> Sodom and Gomorrah and the surrounding towns gave themselves up to sexual immorality and perversion. They serve as an example of those who suffer the punishment of eternal fire.

This verse confirms the sexual immorality of Sodom and Gomorrah. However, since the story of these two ancient cities is about violent acts, Jude 7 is not of great value in talking about committed same-sex relationships.

JUDGES 19:1-30

This is an odd story. In verse 22 there is a scene reminiscent of Sodom:

> While they were enjoying themselves, some of the wicked men of the city surrounded the house. Pounding on the door, they shouted to the old man who owned the house, "Bring out the man who came to your house so we can have sex with him."

Even more than the story of Sodom, this is a story of attempted same-sex sexual abuse, and not helpful when considering the Bible's position on monogamous, devoted gay relationships.

SLAVES, WOMEN, AND GAY PEOPLE

It is not enough to think of the above biblical texts (even the clearer ones) in isolation. We need to look for related principles and themes in Scripture.

One of the most helpful resources I've found is William J. Webb's book *Slaves, Women & Homosexuality*. Webb writes about what he calls the "redemptive-movement hermeneutic."[9] It's a way of noticing the Bible's progression on important issues.

My simple summary of Webb's insights is this: God took the people of the Bible where they were. Through Scripture, God nudged his people toward life as it should be lived, but he knew he couldn't jerk them immediately into a mature Judeo-Christian ethic. Here's the way Webb put it:

Scripture, as with a good teaching methodology, is designed to take people from where they are (the known) and help them move to a foreseeable future (the unknown) that has enough continuity with the present so that they can actually find their way into the preferred future. . . . The educational receptivity of the audience affected the level at which their human and divine instructors could teach. . . . Good teachers, then, set the level of the instructional material at the level of their students. A lower level of delivery might encompass the basics, but it will often not have the advantage of development or refinement that one might like.[10]

What God said about important social and spiritual matters was often in stark contrast to the messages his people were getting from their culture. So God took them at their level of understanding and moved them in the right direction.

Webb takes that principle and applies it to three important topics: slavery, the role of women, and same-sex intimacy. He makes a really important observation about those three:

The bulk of the biblical texts concerning slaves and women move in a less restrictive or freeing direction relative to their original culture. They may not go as far as we might like, but they clearly move in a liberalizing direction relative to the setting in which they were given. On the other hand, the homosexual texts move in a conservative or restrictive direction relative to the original culture.[11]

In other words, Scripture moved the people of God to look at slaves with a progressively more loving spirit than others in their culture did, and increasingly to accept women as far more valuable than what was reflected in their culture. On same-sex intimacy, however, Scripture was not as accepting as the surrounding culture was. While the culture was somewhat permissive about same-sex relationships, Scripture was strictly prohibitive.

Webb also notes the progression within the Bible itself toward freedom for slaves and the elevation of the role of women. Again, he makes a distinction between women and slavery on the one hand and same-sex intimacy on the other. Regarding women and slavery, Webb writes that while the New Testament never speaks with the clarity we would like about these subjects, there is a clear progression within its pages that leads us as Christians to condemn slavery and to affirm women.

With same-sex intimacy, however, the same restrictive tone we find in the Old Testament appears again and is reinforced in the New Testament. Webb writes, "When one comes to the New Testament, there is no softening of Scripture's negative assessment of homosexuality found in the Old Testament."[12] Thus, Webb concludes: "If we talk about the homosexuality texts . . . we discover a different kind of movement. . . . The Christian community must continue its negative assessment of homosexual behavior and restrict such activities within the church, even if society at large does not."[13]

So a new day for women and slaves was, by the time the New Testament closed, still emerging. Yet again, there is no indication in the New Testament of a "new day" regarding same-sex intimacy. Nothing even hints at contradicting the Old Testament texts that prohibit same-sex intimacy.

Holy Scripture was written in a place and time very different from our own. Yet the contexts are not so different that the Bible does not speak to us. I believe the plain reading, even of complicated texts, limits the celebration of sex to the covenant marriage of a man and a woman.

PART THREE

THE WAY FORWARD

CHAPTER SEVEN

WHAT SHOULD A SAME-SEX ATTRACTED CHRISTIAN DO?

I'D LIKE TO SPEAK a quick personal word here to same-sex attracted members of a church family: there are a number of compassionate people in your church who want to help you but don't know how to go about it. So help us. Find a minister or church leader you trust, tell your story, and share what you need from the church. Don't give up on us. Help us help you. You can assist us with our own battles with pride, egotism, and hypocrisy. You can help us with our own sexual struggles. We are in this together. I cannot know your perspective, but I can walk alongside you.

Now to the practical implications of what I advocate here.

IMPORTANT DISTINCTIONS

I want to draw a distinction between (1) sexual attraction or orientation and (2) sexual behavior. Same-sex attraction is simply some level of physical attraction to people of the same sex. When same-sex attraction is "strong enough, durable enough, and persistent enough for them to feel that they are *oriented* toward the same sex," Mark Yarhouse describes it as "homosexual orientation."[1]

There are a number of Christians who acknowledge their same-sex attraction, and even what Yarhouse calls a homosexual orientation, who do not assume a gay identity and do not engage in same-sex sexual intimacy. Yarhouse, a therapist, suggests that "talking to people in specific terms about their attractions is more helpful than presuming that an identity has already been shaped around these attractions."[2] These distinctions are particularly important in this chapter, for here I suggest options I believe are available for same-sex attracted Christians.

Let me also note another important distinction: the difference between celibacy and chastity or abstinence. This actually seems to me to be an important distinction. Celibacy seems to be a spiritual gift granted to some who have a particular calling to serve the church only. Abstinence, or chastity, is a choice made to conform to biblical guidelines for sexual intercourse. Celibacy is "foregoing marriage and genital sexual intimacy for the purpose of a special service to God and others."[3] Abstinence is "not a particular calling for certain persons, but an ethical ideal for all who are not married."[4]

Given those distinctions, let's move to what I believe is the best option for the same-sex attracted person who desires to be true to God's intentions as communicated in Scripture: abstinence.

ABSTINENCE

I believe the appropriate choice for Christ-followers who are same-sex attracted is the same as that for unmarried straight people—abstinence.

I like the way Richard B. Hays expressed it: "While Paul regarded celibacy as a charisma, he did not therefore suppose that those lacking the charisma were free to indulge their sexual desires outside marriage. Heterosexually oriented persons are also called to abstinence from sex unless they marry (1 Cor. 7:8-9)."[5]

An abstinent gay person is one who recognizes an attraction to persons of the same sex but does not act on that attraction. That is no more sinful than an unmarried straight person recognizing an attraction to a member of the opposite sex, yet choosing not to engage in a sexual relationship outside of marriage. Remember: Jesus himself was tempted but did not sin (see Hebrews 4:15).

It has been widely noted that to encourage abstinence of gay people is not to ask anything we don't also ask of single straight people. Yet others have pointed out that for the single straight person there is always the hope out there that, if he or she wants to, they might find a mate and be able to marry. Admittedly, the Traditional teaching of the church does not offer marriage as a potential option to the person who is same-sex attracted.

Whether or not fulfillment is possible through a life of Christian abstinence seems to depend on the one speaking or writing. Many see absolutely no redeeming aspects of gay abstinence, even pointing to what they believe to be devastating psychological results from attempts to remain abstinent. James Brownson predicts dire consequences for those who experience same-sex attraction and choose not to act on it:

> The distinction between orientation and behavior will probably condemn those gay and lesbian Christians who embrace traditionalist teaching to a lifetime of inner turmoil and tension, even if they control their behavior, and even if they do not regularly experience overwhelmingly lustful thoughts. . . . The emotional burden imposed explicitly or implicitly by traditionalists on contemporary gays and lesbians . . . creates a profoundly difficult and duplicitous message of acceptance laced with rejection.[6]

There are those who believe the idea of gay persons remaining abstinent is absolutely ridiculous. John Shore writes, "It's an argument that could only make sense to a brain-dead person. It's just too lame for words."[7]

Yet all reflections on abstinence for gay people are not so condescending or dismal. Some even speak and write of the fulfilling lives of abstinent gay people. In *Washed and Waiting*, Wesley Hill explains his decision, as a gay man, to remain abstinent. He acknowledges his struggle of "my homosexuality, my exclusive attraction to other men, my grief over it and my repentance, my halting effort to live fittingly in the grace of Christ and the power of the Spirit." Yet he says,

> I am . . . slowly but surely, learning to view that journey—of struggle, failure, repentance, restoration, renewal in joy, and persevering, agonized obedience—as what it looks like for the Holy Spirit to be transforming me on the basis of Christ's cross and His Easter morning triumph over death.[8]

Hill has found fulfillment in his identity in Christ. Here are his words:

> Imitating Jesus; conforming my thoughts, beliefs, desires, and hopes to his; sharing his life; embracing his gospel's no to gay sex—I become *more* fully alive, not less. . . . To give up gay sex is to say yes to full, rich, abundant life.[9]

A number of contemporary theologians have reminded us that Jesus showed us what it is to be truly and fully human. If that is true, and I believe it is, then sexuality is not nearly as important to being human as our culture would suggest. Life can be full and rich, even without sex. After all, Jesus practiced abstinence.

Debra Hirsch experienced a dramatic conversion to faith in Jesus after drug abuse and sex with both men and women. She now holds a Traditional view of sexuality, but has invested herself in ministry to people on the margins of the Christian faith, including those who are gay. Hirsch writes:

> I am thankful that Jesus was a single man . . . because in him we find the redemption of celibacy, and therefore of singleness. And as many of my dear friends (both gay and straight) are walking the celibate path, this gives them a deeper insight and appreciation of what Jesus experienced.[10]

Stephen R. Holmes says, "To prove that sexual activity is not necessary to a well-lived life, we need to say only one word, 'Jesus.'"[11]

For many, chastity is a spiritual discipline that is part of an overall process of sanctification, or more simply put, becoming holy. Sexual restraint has been recognized throughout the Christian centuries as a means of opening ourselves up to the Spirit's work in us. In today's sex-crazed culture, abstinence sounds almost ludicrous, but we cannot allow ourselves to be shaped by what the Bible calls "the world," no matter how archaic the notion of chastity seems. Romans 12:2 reads, "Do not conform to the pattern of this world, but be transformed by the renewing of your mind. Then you will be able to test and approve what God's will is—his good, pleasing and perfect will."[12]

Notice that God's will is described as "good, pleasing and perfect." The sexual guidelines given to us by God (sex is to be celebrated within the covenant marriage of a man and a woman) are not given by a spoilsport, but by a loving Father who understands and desires what is best for us. Ed Shaw, a celibate, Christian gay man, writes, "We have, unintentionally, made Jesus' way sound like a bad deal rather than the best way for any human life to be lived—which it is!"[13]

Shaw doesn't deny the costly nature of his choice to remain chaste, but he also decries the obsession with self-gratification that seems to characterize so many of us. He speaks of the spiritual value of sacrifice, believing that Jesus himself, as a single man, "teaches us that suffering for a good purpose is not to be avoided but embraced."[14]

SUPPORTING THOSE WHO REMAIN ABSTINENT

If we are going to ask gay persons to remain abstinent, the church owes them a great deal of grace and support. I feel the weight of this truth as a pastor. I understand that my position in this discussion could discourage same-sex attracted people from being part of the congregation I serve, and that is distressing for me. I honestly want us to be welcoming. Besides that, I can only imagine how difficult it would be to remain abstinent. The very least I feel we can do as a church is to offer unconditional love to people whose sexual attraction is to their own sex. If we don't do that, we will hurt and alienate lots of people and we will suffer a great loss ourselves. We will be richer as a congregation if we truly embrace same-sex attracted people.

As a church, that means we will have to deliberately include same-sex attracted members of our church family in our social events, ministry opportunities, and discipleship groups. We are going to have to get over our debilitating fears and sinful prejudices and welcome same-sex attracted people in ways that will surprise them.

Kevin DeYoung echoes that: "If we ask the single Christian to be chaste, we can only ask them to carry that cross in community. . . . If everything in Christian community revolves around being married with children, we should not be surprised when singleness sounds like a death sentence."[15]

In light of these helpful words from DeYoung, churches need to be careful about articulating the oft-heard vision to "reach young families." When we say we want to reach young families, what we unintentionally communicate is, "If you are single, we are not trying to reach you." All our churches ought to do an audit to uncover ways we unintentionally and perhaps unknowingly send subtle signals that we are family-friendly but not single-friendly.

The premise of this book is that churches must be welcoming. That goes far beyond shaking hands in a worship service. Whether or not we truly are welcoming will be determined by how at home same-sex attracted people feel around our tables, in our Sunday school classes, and on our mission trips.

A number of gay people openly embrace the Christian faith, as do many straight people who live together outside of marriage yet get up on Sunday morning and go to church. A gay Christian said to Philip Yancey, "We get such hatred and rejection from the church that there's no reason to bother with church at all unless you really do believe the gospel is true."[16]

As a married, straight man who gets to celebrate the gift of sexual intimacy within my marriage, I cannot understand what it means to remain abstinent. Furthermore, I cannot claim to know what it is like to be a same-sex attracted Christian. Yet I do appreciate the tenacity that so many demonstrate—a willingness to remain engaged with the church despite how some church people speak of them. And I want to do my best to be both fair and compassionate, despite my Traditional position.

CHAPTER EIGHT

WE CAN'T JUST SING KUMBAYA FOREVER

As much as many of us would like to avoid this conversation, avoidance is becoming increasingly untenable. Eventually most of us will have to address the topic of sexuality.

Many are doing so right now. Denominations are debating this topic with an intensity unseen since the divisions over slavery in the mid-nineteenth century. Churches are wrestling with this topic with a fury unseen since, well, maybe ever.

And this is not going away. Countless communities of faith are now asking if they should address the topics covered in this book. If so, how? And when?

DENOMINATIONAL STRUCTURE

How your congregation deals with this topic will depend on your denominational identity, of course. Some churches are autonomous and decide matters such as this on their own, independent of a denominational hierarchy. Other churches are dependent on their denominational bodies for official positions on topics such as this. If your congregation is not autonomous, you will have to translate parts of the following section for your particular situation.

SHOULD A CHURCH ISSUE A POSITION STATEMENT?

Again, if your church is part of a denominational structure in which position statements are made at the denominational level, you will need to translate this section for your own circumstances. When I refer to a church or congregation, for example, you might want to substitute denomination. Of course, some would contend that a denomination's identity should be broad enough to include congregations across a wide spectrum and would intentionally avoid taking a position as a denomination. Other denominations are taking intentional positions. My intent here is to address local churches and trust readers to make appropriate application to denominational bodies.

Churches across the country are deciding whether or not to issue position statements on the matter of same-sex relationships. The idea of issuing a position statement has elicited deeply emotional responses. Congregations have been divided, with some wanting to take a Traditional stance, with others wanting to issue an Affirming statement, and with still others hoping their church will not say anything at all about it. David Gushee calls these three groups the traditionalists, the revisionists, and the avoiders.

Gushee writes:

> Everywhere I go, I run into three different kinds of responses to the LGBT issue: . . . *Avoiders* want to evade the subject for a wide variety of reasons, including genuine convictional uncertainty, fear of hurting people and fear of conflict and schism. . . .
>
> Avoiders are often quite intense in their desire to avoid the issue altogether, often linked to their responsibility for holding institutions together or keeping their jobs. . . . Whether rightly or not, the LGBT issue has become the hottest of hot-button issues in our generation, so ultimately *avoidism* proves insufficient. Everyone will have to figure out what they will think and do about this.[1]

I believe Gushee is right.

In October 2017, the Church Clarity website (churchclarity .org) was launched. On their home page the leaders of this initiative declare "churches should be clear about their policies" on same-sex matters, for "ambiguity is harmful and clarity is reasonable." They plan to give a score to churches and publish the scores on their site. Lots of people are skeptical of the intent behind this initiative and predict that after the "scoring" there will be public pressure on churches to score "Affirming." Yet, I have to agree that there is a lot to be said for clarity.

Avoidance of a decision and position on this matter is no longer an option for churches.

YOU CAN BE EITHER PROACTIVE OR REACTIVE

My sense is that a church is likely either to take a proactive position now or a reactive position later. In an old ad campaign for Fram oil filters, an auto mechanic would say, "You can pay me now . . . or pay me later." The message was that the consumer could spend a little money now or a whole lot of money after a catastrophe. The same is true for churches and positions on this debate. We can make a decision now . . . or make it later.

The matter is exploding in divisive ways among congregations all over the country. Without having given the topic prayerful thought, churches are responding on the fly to the following:

- requests for same-sex weddings in the facilities
- requests for ministers to perform same-sex weddings (inside or away from the church facilities)
- requests for the public dedication of children adopted by same-sex couples

- requests from potential ministers to know the position of the congregation, and vice versa
- the call for ordination of gay people in same-sex relationships
- the nomination of beloved gay church members to leadership positions

Congregations are often taken by surprise and then forced to make big decisions amid the heat of controversy instead of through a prayerful, reasoned, calm process.

I believe it is likely that most congregations will address the matter now proactively or down the road reactively. And a reactive response will have a name or names attached to it. It will be personal. It will be in response to a situation involving a beloved member of your church family. A proactive conversation is much less emotional and much less divisive than a reactive conversation.

NEUTRALITY IS NOT AN OPTION

Sexuality has become a defining topic in our society. Neutrality is no more an option.

This is one of the biggest cultural discussions of our generation. For a church to remain silent on this violates our call to be salt and light in the world. Churches that choose to isolate themselves and not even engage in dialogue about this topic will become increasingly irrelevant.

I believe people deserve to know where their ministers stand on this topic too. It would be irresponsible for any Christian leader or thinker to not have an understanding of the issues or articulate a position. His or her position should be taken humbly and compassionately, for sure, but he or she should be able to state a position nonetheless.

Any unwillingness on the part of a Christian leader or thinker to come down on one side of this debate seems fainthearted. Any willingness to come down uninformed on one side of this debate, however, is reckless.

A GUIDING PRINCIPLE IS NEEDED

Without a guiding principle, future decisions about issues such as who the church will consider for ministers, who can be married and by whom, who is eligible for leadership, and so on, will be made without direction from the congregation.

In any church, the healthiest processes involve the congregation speaking to major concerns, giving direction for their leaders and ministers to follow when tough questions arise. Whether it is future search teams, business meetings, or leadership discussions, it's critical for the church to clarify its direction, at least in a general sense.

Perhaps this is a good time to talk about whether this is a conversation for a church to have in its interim period between pastors (for those denominations who have interim periods). If there is a clear and large majority of the congregation that agrees on this topic, I believe the interim period between pastors is a good time to make the decision. A decision gives direction to the search committee so that they can find a pastoral candidate who is compatible with the congregation. It also is fair to the potential pastor. For one thing, he or she will not have to come in and tackle this issue. For another thing, it helps the potential pastor know what he or she is getting into. The pastor has compatibility questions to answer as well.

However, if the congregation is not clear as to how it will handle people who are in same-sex relationships, and if there is no obvious consensus, then it is hard to imagine such a congregation coming to a healthy conclusion on this topic without a pastor in place. While I believe a pastor should not hand down an edict on a topic as important as this, a pastor's guidance will be critical if a diverse church is going to handle difficult discussions and come to some sort of conclusion without splintering.

YOUR CHURCH CAN MODEL COMPASSION AND TRUTH

With so many churches embracing an unqualified affirmation of same-sex sexual practice, and so many others taking the route of hostile condemnation of gay people, you can do your best to find and model the balance.

If same-sex intimacy is indeed less than God's intention for his people, then we have a responsibility to offer a compelling perspective both to those inside and outside the church who are struggling to find an answer, whether that answer is theoretical or personal.

This includes, of course, the next generation. This gives us an opportunity to explore and declare anew our commitment to the authority of Scripture, as we understand it, under the leadership of the Holy Spirit.

This is a defining topic not only in society, but also in many ways within churches. If the church has issued a position statement on the matter, it is likely that the position statement will help potential church members decide to join. I've been told by people looking for a church home that they want to know where churches stand regarding this topic.

There are a number of churches and church leaders who prefer not to make statements on same-sex relationships. Some simply hate the potential for division. Some suggest that any statements on this subject are likely to be misinterpreted no matter how they are written. Some want to protect their congregations from the pain of disagreement. Some ministers recognize differences on this topic between themselves and a majority of the congregation and would rather not have those differences and disconnects come to light. Some just fear conflict.

Others simply disagree, based on principle, with a church taking a position. Debra Hirsch suggests that if we are going to have a statement on same-sex sexual behavior we ought to have a statement on every other debatable ethical issue.[2]

Hirsch's point is well taken. My opinion, however, is that this is such a defining conversation in our day that a position cannot be avoided. It should not be the kind of position that says, "Unless you agree with this you cannot be part of our church," and it should not reflect poorly on churches who take different positions. However, it should reflect the majority view of the congregation.

I certainly believe a statement by a church should address the broad Christian view of sexuality, not just same-sex intimacy. Yet I believe a position statement by individual congregations is not only helpful—it is essential.

Of course, for all those congregations in the broad middle, this will be a difficult conversation. Even a difficult conversation, however, is better than having a statement handed down by authoritarian church leaders, or having church leaders assume (often incorrectly) what members of the congregation think. As risky and painful as the conversation might be, if the conversation is handled well, in the long run your church will be stronger for it.

CHAPTER NINE

WELCOMING BUT NOT AFFIRMING AND MUTUALLY TRANSFORMING

MANY OF US GENUINELY struggle to find the balance between fighting for too much and standing for too little. Speaking with gentle clarity about our convictions is appropriate, even necessary. Yet, some of us would have to admit that our response to same-sex attracted people has not always been Christlike. Balance is an appropriate and ambitious goal.

CLARITY AND INFREQUENCY

The Bible speaks with clarity and infrequency on same-sex intimacy. In Romans 1, 1 Timothy 1, and 1 Corinthians 6, I believe Scripture speaks clearly. But the Bible doesn't denounce same-sex intimacy over and over.

That clarity and infrequency should be the stance of a church. We should speak with as much clarity as we reasonably can. And yet we should speak with infrequency. This should not be an ongoing, dominating, identifying theme. A church should address it and then move on.

Let me be clear: I'm not suggesting the issue is a one-and-done. And the topic should never be considered off-limits. Yet, a church should follow the lead of the Bible we love and not make this a central, defining matter for the church. Pastors should not make this a recurring theme of sermons. Our passion must be God's mission. Our theme must be God's grace, which is mentioned in the New Testament with great frequency—one hundred and fourteen times.

On the other hand, if you were to remove the singular references in Romans 1, 1 Timothy 1, and 1 Corinthians 6, you're left with nothing of real substance in the Bible regarding same-sex intimacy to talk about. Granted, the topic of same-sex intimacy was not nearly as dominant in culture in biblical days as it is today, but one hundred and fourteen to three is still a pretty significant ratio.

Out of respect for the authority of Holy Scripture, I believe we should not speak with less clarity than that with which the Bible speaks about same-sex intimacy. Also out of respect for the authority of Holy Scripture, I believe we should not speak with more frequency than the Bible does.

GRACE AND TRUTH

John introduced us to Jesus in the opening words in the Bible's book that bears his name. He described Jesus as the one who came from the Father, full of grace and truth. Grace and truth must be our guiding principles when it comes to dealing with any moral issue, including sexuality.

I believe the unambiguous message taken from a plain reading of the texts is that sexual intimacy is intended by God only for the covenant, marriage relationship of a man and a woman who have said, "For better or worse, till death do us part." I believe same-sex intimate relationships are clearly outside those God-given boundaries. That, I believe, is the truth.

Then there's grace. Grace is God's unconditional, undeserved, unlimited, unrelenting love. Grace means our place in God's heart and our value in God's eyes are not determined by our decisions.

Grace means, in the words of Philip Yancey, "*There is nothing we can do to make God love us more . . . [and] nothing we can do to make God love us less.*"[1] There is nothing good you can do to earn one ounce more of God's love than you already have, for he loves you infinitely. And there is nothing bad you can do to forfeit one ounce of God's love, for he loves you unconditionally.

Of course grace does not mean our choices are unimportant. On the contrary, the Bible sets a high standard for morality, ethics, and spirituality. A dominant theme in Scripture is that the choices we make matter to God, shape our lives, and impact people around us.

There's not a word in the definition of grace about leniency, indulgence, enabling, anything goes, a wink and a nod, or turning a blind eye to obvious wrongdoing. In fact, the short New Testament book of Jude warns against people who "pervert the grace of our God into a license for immorality" (Jude 4).

Years ago, I asked someone to step aside from church leadership for a season due to behavioral choices inconsistent with our congregation's values. I was confronted by a couple of that person's friends and asked how I could preach grace so often and then turn around and penalize this person. "That's judgmentalism, not grace," they protested. Wasn't I preaching one thing and practicing another? My answer was and is that grace is neither cheap nor lenient.

Unconditional love is not undemanding love. Christian love is challenging, purifying, and sometimes tough. Again, grace simply means that our value in God's eyes and our place in God's heart are not determined by whether we meet God's standards. Grace does not mean anything goes.

And we are to extend grace to those we differ with. 1 Peter 4:10 says we are to be "stewards of God's grace."

Again, grace is God's unconditional, undeserved, unlimited, unrelenting love toward us. But we are also to extend grace to each other. There is a beautiful line from Joseph R. Cooke: "Grace is the face that love wears when it meets imperfection."[2] Grace includes the will to embrace those with whose opinions we disagree, even those with whose choices we disagree.

So that is the balance: truth and grace. When all is said and done, I hope people will remember that you and I declared truth because we were compelled to do so, and we extended grace because we were thrilled to do so.

Now we turn to another popular phrase, a phrase that seems to be our best option at balancing grace and truth.

WELCOMING BUT NOT AFFIRMING

This is the position being embraced by a number of centrist evangelicals. The phrase comes from the title of a book by the late evangelical scholar Stanley Grenz, who described his position like this:

> My goal is to indicate that the mandate we have received from our Lord calls the church to welcome homosexual persons on the same basis that all persons are to be welcomed. But this same mandate prohibits the church from condoning same-sex behavior as well as same-sex sexual unions.[3]

I believe Grenz got it right. Simply put, I believe we should welcome all followers of Jesus who want to be part of our church families. I want to declare it once more: I welcome anyone and everyone to the circle.

I also believe we are to make clear the biblical message about sexual intimacy—that it is to be expressed only within the marriage between a man and a woman. I further believe that spiritual leadership should be reserved for those whose life choices reflect biblical values. Thus I cannot affirm people in same-sex relationships for leadership roles in the church.

MEMBERSHIP

Of course, there are those churches that are not welcoming. They would restrict membership (and perhaps even worship and fellowship) to those either in a straight marriage or living a completely abstinent life. That is not an appealing option for me.

For one thing, membership as most churches practice it (voting people in, maintaining membership rolls, and such) is not in the Bible as I can find. Therefore, we have to make decisions about church membership based on New Testament principles without explicit guidance from Scripture.

More importantly, if a church has not made any particular moral issue a qualifier or disqualifier for membership up to this point, then it would be very difficult for that church to justify making sexuality a litmus test for membership now. As an example, if your church has not singled out any specific moral issue as a qualifier or disqualifier for membership; has not asked if straight, unmarried couples are living together; has not asked if people are willing to stop smoking or get help for their addictions; has not asked people if they cheat on their tests or tax returns—well then it would seem wrong for your church to make this the issue that you use to keep people out.

I am certain there will be those in evangelical churches who agree with my Traditional stance on same-sex relationships and yet who will disagree with me on allowing gay people in same-sex relationships to be members. I appreciate that position. However, if you are not yet willing to grant membership to persons who are in same-sex relationships, I ask you to consider the following:

- Does your church really want to single out this matter as the disqualifier from membership? If so, what is the biblical rationale for that? Personal discomfort with same-sex intimacy is not a valid justification for denying membership to gay people.

- What if this were your son or daughter, grandson or granddaughter? If your son or daughter, or grandson or granddaughter, were living a life you didn't agree with, wouldn't you still want somebody in some church to put an arm around your son or daughter and say, "I cannot affirm your choices but I love you unconditionally, and you are welcome here"? Would it not be wonderful for your church to be the kind of place where our own sons and daughters are welcomed, not shunned, even when we don't affirm their lifestyles?

But, someone might ask, if we welcome people in same-sex relationships, won't we be endorsing bad behavior? Won't we be condoning sin?

Nope. Welcoming people and condoning sin are two different things. Jesus welcomed sinners. Moreover, your church has a long history of welcoming people who sin by choice rather often. If you don't believe me, look around the room next time you're in worship!

It's a good thing that churches welcome people whose choices are often sinful, for our best opportunity to help with each other's transformation is if we are praying, worshiping, serving, and maturing together. That is true no matter what our greatest struggle is.

A church's membership is enriched when it comes to believe, "We are all in need of transformation and we are dependent on God's Spirit for that work; our hope for eternity is in Jesus instead of our own goodness; we are accountable to each other for our ongoing spiritual maturation; and the purpose of this church is not to make me happy."

Church membership is not about privilege. It's about commitment to common values, devotion to a shared mission, and responsibility to one another. Membership ought to imply a willingness to undergo ongoing transformation with others on the same journey. Church membership should require from anyone a commitment to increasing holiness through spiritual disciplines and the power of God's Spirit with the support of the community.

Implied in church membership is the sacrifice of discipleship, not an opportunity to be coddled or to have one's every decision affirmed. Richard Hays wrote that his close friend Gary, who experienced same-sex attraction, wrote a final letter to Hays before Gary's death. Gary advocated for including same-sex attracted people in the church family, yet added: "Anyone who joins such a community should know that it is a place of transformation, of discipline, learning, and not merely a place to be comforted and indulged."[4]

So, would declaring that your church is welcoming result in an influx of gay people? Probably not. While some would be saddened by that, and others not, the fact remains that a Welcoming but Not Affirming position would not result in a number of gay men and women joining your church.

Candidly, a Welcoming but Not Affirming position could mean most gay Christians would not choose to be members of your congregation. Welcoming but Not Affirming feels non-welcoming to many people who are gay. Many same-sex attracted people appreciate Traditionalists' sincere insistence that they are welcome, even though their behavior is not affirmed. Yet, they still find it far too uncomfortable to participate in a congregation in which they feel like second-class members.[5]

If your church were to take the same position that I have taken—Welcoming but Not Affirming and Mutually Transforming—it would not be without its challenges. I have to acknowledge the unique combination of compassion and courage that is required to continue to teach what the Bible says about sexuality while making everyone feel valued. We will have to go out of our way to make sure "All are welcome here" is more than a line in a song. Living out the welcoming side of Welcoming but Not Affirming could be challenging for some, and it might get messy. I simply believe we have no choice but to give it our very best.

LEADERSHIP

So, I am welcoming when it comes to membership. Because I am not Affirming, however, church leadership is a different matter.

Because of the responsibilities and influence that come from the high-profile of leadership in the church, leaders are held to a higher standard than others. James 3:1 reads, "Not many of you should become teachers, my fellow believers, because you know that we who teach will be judged more strictly."

It's true that the church is for broken people. Church is indeed a hospital for sinners, not a hotel for saints. Nevertheless, I believe leadership in the church is reserved for those who have demonstrated spiritual maturity, deep loyalty, and a track record of moral and ethical decisions that reflect the model of Jesus and the demands of Scripture.

Hays says the following about membership versus leadership in the church:

Can homosexual persons be members of the Christian church?
This is rather like asking, "Can envious persons be members
of the church?" (cf. Rom. 1:29) or "Can alcoholics be
members of the church?" De facto, of course, they are. . . .

At the same time, I would argue that the pastoral task
of the church is to challenge self defined homosexual
Christians to reshape their identity in conformity with
the gospel. Those who hold the offices of teaching and
preaching in the church should uphold the biblical standard
and call all who hear to follow. This is a tricky line to
walk, but we do it on many issues.[6]

Conversely, many believe it is disingenuous to welcome
sexually active gay people into the church but deny them the
opportunity to lead. For some, leadership restrictions constitute
a second-class membership.

Nevertheless, I do believe there is biblical justification for
holding higher standards for leadership in the church. I believe
we can and must expect more from our leaders. There are a
number of issues that would disqualify one from spiritual
leadership, including same-sex intimacy. In the twenty-five-plus
years I have been a pastor, I can remember asking two lay
leaders to step down from leadership for sexual immorality;
both were straight.

But why would same-sex sexual behavior be one of the
disqualifiers from leadership? As I understand the New Testament, there are three specific categories of sins that are
treated more seriously than others within the body of Christ:
divisive behavior, sexual sins, and erroneous teachings. These
three are singled out because of the depth of their impact on
both individuals and on the congregation as a whole. I believe
that all three exclude persons from leadership (see
Matthew 18:15-17; Romans 16:17-19; 1 Corinthians 5:1-5, 9-10,

12-13; Ephesians 4:3; 1 Timothy 1:18-20; Titus 1:10-11; Titus 3:9-10).

I could not support ordination for people in same-sex sexual relationships. However, just as I would support a qualified, abstinent, single straight person, I also would support a qualified, abstinent, same-sex attracted man or woman for ordination.

Before we move on from the topic of leadership, let me quickly remind you that a church that decides to welcome people in same-sex relationships into membership but not leadership will then have to define leadership. Is leadership limited to ordination? Does leadership include high-profile positions such as elders, the church council, or Sunday school teachers? Can a gay person in a same-sex relationship serve in any elected leadership role? A congregation must wrestle with these hard questions.

WELCOMING AND MUTUALLY TRANSFORMING

David Fitch offered a term I like: Welcoming and Mutually Transforming.[7] This transformation, of course, is toward the image of Jesus. Fitch's proposal reminds us that (1) we all are broken; and (2) all of us are on the discipleship journey together—not one of us has arrived, and all of us take steps backward and forward along the way. All of us are in need of ongoing transformation.

Tony Campolo, in his article explaining why he changed his mind, said he is "finally ready to call for the full acceptance of Christian gay couples into the Church." He contends, "When we sing the old invitation hymn, 'Just As I Am,' I want us to mean it, and I want my gay and lesbian brothers and sisters to know it is true for them too."[8] That's a gracious sentiment.

However, I also remember the quote attributed to Leighton Ford, "God loves us the way we are, but too much to leave us that way." Transformation means we are not content to live with any of those things in our lives that do not align with God's intentions for us, including but certainly not limited to our sexual practices. All of us are to submit to the transformation that is both possible by God's Spirit and mandated by Scripture.

My favorite term, then, is Welcoming but Not Affirming and Mutually Transforming. That is what I see as the biblical position—reflecting the appropriate emphasis on both grace and truth.

TESTIMONIAL

CALLED TO STAY

Below is the testimony of a pastor whose congregation has remained in their denomination although his congregation is not in agreement with the denomination's decision to endorse same-sex marriage and ordination (deacon, priest, bishop) of persons in non-celibate same-sex relationships (married or otherwise). The situation has resulted in what my pastor friend described as "disappointment, spiritual exhaustion, and a high level of tension."

We are dedicated to the denomination and the historic faith. Like Hosea of old, divorce is not an option for us. Rather, we are called to stay in relationship with the denomination in the hope that God will restore her and use her to glorify himself. Likewise, in all four Gospels Jesus calls us to follow him (Matthew 4:19; Mark 1:17; Luke 5:27; John 1:43), and Jesus remained a Jew and repeatedly went to the Jewish authorities and debated with them even though they rejected his message and ultimately rejected him. As a parish and individuals we are trying to stand firm for the faith within the denomination and perhaps be a light for those who wish to see.

The tone of our church is intentionally positive, proactive, and missional. The focus continues to be to announce and demonstrate the direction and purpose of God in the world through Jesus Christ. We continue to define ourselves according to the call God has placed on our hearts rather than identifying ourselves as against the denomination or any other group. We recognize that the power behind any stance with regard to the denomination is a matter of call. Each of us individually and corporately must discern the path of obedience that God has willed for us. We have discerned a call to stay in the family to provide an example of an authentic identity with our heritage. That being said, we continue to resist the temptation to sit back and let things happen. To be missional is to stand for something, so we seek ways to represent the truth of Jesus Christ in the life and counsels of the church as a fellowship of witness.

At this point in the history of the denomination, we have become very accomplished at listening to ourselves but reasonably deaf to the voices of the other provinces of our communion. Furthermore, the voices of those we choose to hear have effectively deafened us to the voice of Scripture.

What is needed above all else is the spirit of charity. Those who are called to remain in the denomination need to acknowledge and honor the call of those who are called to leave and form a new entity. Likewise, the reformers need to refrain from making assumptions about those who are called to be a witness in the denomination and respect their chosen path of obedience. Although our ecclesiological goals may be different—reformation versus witness—our ultimate goal is the same: to proclaim the gospel in whatever circumstance we find ourselves.

My prayer is that we may be united in our mutual ministry and supportive of one another as we manifest our obedience along the distinct paths to which we are called.

When I say that I am called to stay as a witness, I am not speaking of a passive, go-with-the-flow, I-will-always-be-identified-with-this-denomination kind of stand. My call is political in terms of its ultimate effect, for it is manifested as a counter story that serves to interpret denominational politics. Staying in the denomination calls for an active stand for the gospel at the parish level, the diocesan level, the national church level, and at the level of the culture. Such a public counter story will have results. In the case of the church, either our denomination will see an alternative model for living and embrace it, or the denomination will reject it. But that institutional decision is not the red line. The red line is drawn where I am directed to do something that is against the counsel of Scripture or face the consequences.

TESTIMONIAL

CALLED TO LEAVE

Here you will read a statement from another close pastor-friend whose church left his denomination. The presenting issue was the matter of ordaining LGBTQ candidates, although you will see there were other matters as well.

In our church's process there were larger issues that preceded the denomination's decision to allow for ministers to ordain people in practicing homosexual relationships. Maybe the central issue was the authority of Scripture. . . . Our confessions were placed on the same level as Scripture. . . . All of this opened the door to not only allowing ministers who were practicing homosexual behavior to be ordained, but also to changing the definition of marriage. Previously, marriage had been defined as between a man and a woman. Now that language was stripped.

I believe if our church would have attempted to stay in the denomination, we might have lost maybe half the church. (Ultimately, our church's vote to leave was by a 98 percent margin.) After the denomination's decision of 2010 on the authority of Scripture, which became official in 2011, our elders initiated a year-long process aimed at presenting their thoughts and listening to the congregation. By mid-year, it was clear the congregation would not make peace with what was decided by the denomination. Then, the goal became to unify the church toward what was clearly the desire of most—to leave and move to another denomination. The elders communicated reasons for leaving. I share this because we saw the issues before us as bigger than sexual ethics. Always, the congregation saw the bigger issue especially as having to do with the authority of Scripture.

As we proceeded through the year, almost all were in agreement. Discussions were always respectful and civil. And, yes, there were a few who left because of the direction we were heading, but that was only a handful. Before the end of the year the congregation had decided to communicate its desire to leave the denomination. Below are our reasons for leaving, as communicated to the congregation.

(1) Someone might say to churches like us, who believe this is a step into biblical unfaithfulness, "Aren't you overblowing the need for change? After all, essentials of the faith have not changed." Our answer is that we believe sexual ethics is a very important area of discipleship and obedience. Nevertheless, we believe that, in our time, sexual ethics is one of the main stages on which divergences from essentials are being played out.

Thus, in truth we do find essentials of the faith at risk in this effort to legitimize same-sex practice.

(2) Churches like our church are continually called to explain that they are not like other parts of the denomination that embrace non-orthodox positions. This defensive posture reduces the impact of our ministries and mission.

(3) The denomination has become so divided that our affiliation is now a greater hindrance rather than a benefit for the ministries of our church. We see little hope of overcoming the theological differences at the root of these divisions. As a result of these divided loyalties and the need to address these conflicts, we divert large amounts of time, energy, and finances away from our core ministries. A great deal of pastors' and elders' time and energy is spent networking and strategizing ways to influence the outcome of votes on contentious issues. Again and again, the focus of our leaders is diverted from the ministries and missions of our churches.

Important in our process was not just the decision to leave but how we went about the leaving. Our church believed in the importance of the unity of the body that made this an excruciating decision. We determined that even though we could not maintain an organizational unity, we would nevertheless seek, to the best of our ability, God helping, to maintain a relational unity. We spoke freely to the congregation of our desire to operate in a way that would glorify God. We spoke to the denominational committee working with us in this process of our desire to glorify God in the way we worked together. We encouraged people to not be controlled by anger but by this desire to honor God, even when we might feel we were being mistreated. On the whole, that is how the congregation and its leaders related to the denomination—respectfully, civilly, lovingly, patiently, being "quick to hear, slow to speak, and slow to anger"—as best we could (because certainly we would wrestle with anger at times).

This was essentially a three-year process. It was very stressful. It wore us and me out. Denominations don't let you go easily. The denominational committee working with us likened it to a divorce—and that is probably an apt analogy. After the process was complete, it would be five to six months before I was re-energized, and maybe longer before I was fully recovered.

I can say for us and for me that though it was very difficult, it was worth it. The church and I feel a new freedom. We are now in a denomination that shares our values.

I can also say that making our aim to glorify God in the process was critical to not only a good outcome but also in our seeking to maintain our witness in doing something that hinders our witness. For example, with some of those who were at first reluctant to leave or even against leaving, the fact that we went about the leaving in a way that sought to honor God helped them to come along. It enhanced our unity. I have seen other churches where anger was at the center of communicating and the process was made much more difficult and outcomes were not as good as ours.

I can also say that a good process was important for us—first, coming to unity as leaders; second, presenting the issues to the people as we leaders saw them and then listening to them; and third, taking our time and not hurrying, having many prayer meetings, bathing the whole process in much prayer. Any good process requires discernment about where your people are at. It requires honest, authentic persuasion. I believe our decision being based in bigger issues than sexual ethics alone was critical to everyone coming on board.

I can also say that good communication, skilled communication, and frequent communication were critical.

CHAPTER TEN

WHAT CAN WE DO?

THIS IS NOT MERELY a congregational or denominational matter; it is an individual matter. This is something each one of us must decide for ourselves and a social reality to which each of us must respond. So how can we go about doing that?

For this chapter I want to speak primarily to readers who share my Traditional view of marriage and sexuality.

WE CAN CROSS THE STREET

In today's culture wars it is as if people are standing on opposite sides of a wide street yelling at each other across several lanes of busy traffic. We, you and I, are going to have to cross that street and develop relationships, listen to other people's stories, and share our own. Whether we change anyone's mind or not, it is our call to love our neighbor, and loving our neighbor is impossible from across the street. It's easy to make pronouncements about people from a distance, but I don't know anyone whose life was changed because someone criticized them from afar.

I have found it wonderfully rewarding to sit down and have cordial, candid conversations with same-sex attracted people—not as a crusader, or even a convincer, but as a listener. I have not hidden my position; my convictions about the matter have been clear. But neither did I shame or belittle anyone. I have listened, really listened, to their stories. I have prayed with people who are gay. And I have recognized my own need for ongoing spiritual transformation. Those conversations and relationships have not altered my interpretation of the biblical texts, but whenever I write about same-sex intimacy I see those faces and hear those voices. Because of those faces and voices, this debate over same-sex intimacy is not merely an exercise in exegesis for me. It is personal.

What if you and I were to sit down with someone who is gay and ask a simple question: "How do I represent Jesus to the LGBT community?" I believe our overture would be welcomed by most, and we would learn a great deal.[1]

In fact, many same-sex attracted people long to be welcomed into a Christian community. Granted, non-Affirming feels nonwelcoming to many. However, Andrew Marin's research demonstrates a widespread longing by gay people to be active in churches, if only they will be treated well![2]

"The New Prodigals," chapter three of Marin's book *Us Versus Us*, offers encouraging news for those of us who hold Traditional views of sexuality yet sincerely love same-sex attracted people and lament that so many feel alienated by the church. Results of his research, such as, "76% of LGBT people are open to returning to their religious community and its practices"[3] are cause for genuine hope.

I am unwilling to believe that Traditional churches cannot truly welcome same-sex attracted people. Marin gives us reason to believe that, if we extend kindness, we can maintain long-established sexual values and enjoy the blessing of same-sex attracted people in our church families.

WE CAN CONFESS

So what should we confess? Here are some suggestions:

We can confess the way we have treated gay people. The mistreatment of people who identify as having same-sex attraction is widespread and, frankly, some of it is rooted in the church. A number of young people are being rejected by their families and their congregations. There is a large percentage of gay young people who are runaways and homeless mainly because of the way people around them have treated them.[4]

Some of us church folks have pressured our sons to conform to our culture's view of masculinity and our daughters to fit the feminine image. Some of us have implied to our kids that God loves only straight people. Some of us have warned our children to keep their same-sex attractions a secret lest they shame us.

Some of us have made fun of those who are different. Some have even suggested that those who have suffered with AIDS got what they deserved. Various high-profile Christian leaders, presuming to speak for the rest of us, have blamed natural disasters on the gay community. We have, in subtle and obvious ways, treated gay people as less than.

In *Us Versus Us*, Marin describes the Marin Foundation's "I'm Sorry" campaign. Christians wearing "I'm Sorry" T-shirts and holding signs such as "I'm sorry for how the church has treated you" and "I'm sorry Christians have shunned you" line the streets of gay pride parades and have wonderful conversations with people in the parades. Marin describes the success of his organization's overtures to same-sex attracted people: "As I've now seen firsthand over and over again, one small act of love is all it takes."[5] It's time to confess where appropriate and repent.

We can confess our discomfort. Truth be known, some of the opposition to same-sex intimacy grows not primarily out of a careful study of Scripture, but out of our own discomfort. Some are simply uneasy with the idea of same-sex intimacy and respond with what they pass off as righteous indignation.

We can confess our sins. We can confess our notion that sexual sins are somehow more abhorrent than sins such as greed and pride. It would be helpful for us to acknowledge that the Bible gives a lot more attention to matters of poverty, fairness, the Great Commandment (love people and love God) and the Great Commission (go to all the world) than to the behavior of two people behind closed doors. Of course that doesn't mean we should ignore the Bible's teachings on same-sex intimacy. However, it seems wise for us to place our emphasis where the Bible places its emphasis.

Richard Hays appropriately chastises us: "Some of the most urgent champions of 'biblical morality' on sexual matters become strangely equivocal when the discussion turns to the New Testament's teachings about possessions."[6] We tell the shameful story of same-sex sexual behavior from Sodom and Gomorrah and almost forget what Ezekiel declares as the most condemning sin of those two cities: "Now this was the sin of your sister Sodom: She and her daughters were arrogant, overfed and unconcerned; they did not help the poor and needy" (Ezekiel 16:49).

WE CAN BE PEOPLE OF INTEGRITY

At a men's retreat I heard a story that I understand is fairly widely known. A national men's ministry was holding a stadium event some years ago. A block of rooms in a nearby hotel had been booked for men who would attend the convention. In the morning one of the hotel managers said to the representative who had booked the rooms, "I thought this was a Christian meeting."

"It is!"

"That's interesting. Over half the rooms rented an adult movie last night."

We've all heard the criticism of people like you and me: "They're just a bunch of hypocrites." Well, as frustrating as it is to be painted with such a broad brush, we have to admit that the charge is not completely unfounded.

And is it possible that hyper-critical crusaders against certain sins are compensating for weaknesses of their own? Sometimes that, indeed, seems to be the case. Sometimes righteous indignation is a smokescreen to cover for similar skeletons in that moral crusader's closet.

Let's be people of integrity. Not so that we can be justified in our Pharisaical attacks on people, but so that when we say, "That is wrong," we can do so with a clean conscience and a straight face.

WE CAN TALK TO OUR YOUTH

We can offer a compelling "script" to our youth who experience same-sex attraction. Mark Yarhouse says that much of the gay community is eager to hand a "gay script" to anyone who is experiencing same-sex attraction. Yarhouse says that gay script looks something like this:

- Your true identity, who you really are, is tied to your sexual orientation.
- Your behavior should reflect who you are at your core.
- Thus, you need to join us as a gay person living life as one of us, a member of the gay community.

That, writes Yarhouse, is a compelling script for someone who is confused and looking for clarity, and/or feeling rejected yet longing to feel included.[7]

Yarhouse makes the point that by either not talking about this matter or talking about it in abrupt, dismissive language ("Don't ask questions; just live right!"), we are not helping our youth make important decisions. If we don't get serious about this, and if we don't offer what Yarhouse calls a "compelling script," we are writing off scores of young adults. Yarhouse reminds us of how important it is to help Jesus-followers understand our identity in Christ. We can remind people that same-sex attraction is part of some people's experience, but that is not what defines them (or us). Rather, our identity in Jesus is that which should determine how we view ourselves.[8]

We cannot simply and naively demand that those with same-sex attraction change. They might comply outwardly with our expectations but they might also die inwardly or secretly pursue their passions in same-sex relationships.

We can, however, help same-sex attracted young people have a sense of identity. We can both teach and model an identity in Christ that is compelling and life-transforming. We can and should declare "freedom in Christ" without shaming and shunning those who do not experience such freedom. We owe that to those among us; they are "our own." We must make sure our young people who express their same-sex attraction know they are "our people."

I understand and lament that the position I'm taking might not encourage same-sex attracted teenagers to speak up at our church. I honestly hope and pray that my Traditional position on same-sex intimacy and marriage will not discourage teens or anyone else from being willing to discuss their struggles with me or others in the church. I want my young Christian brothers and sisters to know that in our church they are among family, that our church is a safe place, and that if they will stick around and help people like me wrestle with our stuff, we'll help them wrestle with theirs.

I will not affirm same-sex intimacy as a viable alternative, for I believe that would not be the loving thing to do. Yet I will plead with teens who are attracted to those of the same sex to remain engaged in the church even though we are so awkward when it comes to talking about this topic. And I will ask them—just as I ask those attracted to the opposite sex—to remain sexually pure from that day on, to abstain until married. I will try to offer a compelling, Christ-centered "script."

Remember, I'm talking about our sons, daughters, grandsons, and granddaughters. And I will say to them, "In this, your church, you can live out your holy identity in Christ and inspire the rest of us as we deal with our own issues." I believe this is part of what it means to be Welcoming but Not Affirming and Mutually Transforming.

Ralph Longshore wrote about a teenage girl who came to a pastor's office one day. After she was sure she could trust the pastor, she admitted that she was only fifteen years old and already a mother. She had become pregnant at age fourteen. The father had stayed around for only a short while. For several months, she wanted to die. She confided in the pastor that had it not been for her baby, she would have taken her own life.

"Do you think God can forgive me?" she asked. The pastor spent time assuring her of God's forgiveness, and showed her from the Bible the promises and examples of his grace.

Finally she asked, "Can the church accept me?"

"Can God forgive me?" and "Can the church accept me?" are two different questions. So the pastor took the matter to the church. When the people of the church were gathered, the pastor simply said that a teenage girl had come to him. He explained that she had made some sinful choices, was in trouble, and wanted to be forgiven. He gave no name. He shared no details. He simply said a teenage girl had made some bad decisions and wanted to know if the church would accept her.

Parents quietly asked themselves, "Is this my child he's talking about?" Grandparents wondered, "Is that our grand-daughter?" All were convinced that if this happened to be their child or grandchild, they would want the rest of the church to be merciful and forgiving. And they all agreed they would love her no matter what she'd done.

So when the pastor introduced the girl to the church, she was overwhelmed by the mercy and forgiveness that she found there. For they all had realized that they or their families could have been in those shoes.[9]

Let's change that story to the story of a young man or woman who comes to the pastor and says, "I am attracted to people of the same sex" or "I've engaged in a same-sex rela-tionship." Let's imagine the pastor coming back to the congre-gation and asking if we are willing to embrace that young man or woman. Might we wonder if the young person were our son or daughter, grandson or granddaughter? Would we embrace him or her? I certainly hope so. It is imperative that we be compassionate and make sure that our youth know they are "our people," no matter what.

WE CAN BE CONSISTENT

I choose not to perform the weddings of people of the same sex, and have turned down one invitation to do that (though I was honored to be asked). I also choose not to perform the weddings of straight couples who are living together. I ask that they separate between the time they ask me to perform their ceremony and the day of the wedding. If they agree, then I gladly marry them.

I say that to say that I do not intend to single out same-sex attracted people in any discriminatory way. So whether the matter is membership or leadership, let's be sure we are applying biblical standards for sexuality fairly, regardless of sexual orientation. Let's make sure we have the same expectations of people whether they are gay or straight, and let's be very clear about that. The very least we can do is be consistent in our moral convictions.

WE CAN CELEBRATE CHRISTIAN MARRIAGE

We can celebrate and work hard to strengthen Christian marriage. Our culture needs for us to model an attractive and compelling view of marriage and biblical sexuality as God designed it. Husbands and wives also need the intimacy and genuine love that only marriage as God intended it can offer. And if we have children at home, they need to see our love. Our children need to see love expressed between us so that they can know that the physical relationship God planned for marriage between a man and a women really is beautiful and worth waiting for.

Dorothy Day wrote in her autobiography about her parents' relationship that she never saw any signs of romantic, passionate love between her parents. That fact made what she was hearing about premarital relationships seem all the more alluring.[10]

Think about it. A teenager is growing up in a home where Mom and Dad don't spend time together and don't ever show affection to each other. The teen goes to a movie where he or she sees a couple (gay or straight) who barely know each other, but they cannot keep their hands off each other. On their first date the couple in the movie jump into a steamy bed. They have a relationship that sizzles.

That teenager then compares what he or she has seen on the screen with the stale, boring relationship he or she has seen at home between a married man and woman. Which do you think this teenager will see as the more desirable? Chances are, when that teenager gets the opportunity, he or she is going to experiment with what was seen on the screen because what the teenager has seen at home isn't all that appealing.

Moms and dads, let your kids know you love each other. They need it. It will do them good to see affection expressed between their parents. And it ought to be a lot of fun for Mom and Dad too!

Our cries for family values ring hollow when the model we present is not compelling. Let's strengthen the family as God designed it.

WE CAN BE HUMBLE

We can be sure that our prophetic role in culture is tempered by humility. We Christians ought to be salt and light in our culture. We ought to have a prophetic voice in our world, speaking against injustice and immorality. I don't believe we should confine our convictions to our church buildings.

Our prophetic role, however, always ought to be tempered by humility and a recognition that it is wrong to rail piously against the evil in others' lives while conveniently ignoring the evil in our own. In fact, Jesus spoke of the planks in our own eyes.

So many actions of churches and self-appointed Christian spokespersons come across as egotistically hypocritical. It's helpful to remember Galatians 6:1, "If someone falls into sin, forgivingly restore him, saving your critical comments for yourself. *You* might be needing forgiveness before the day's out" (*The Message*).

Many of us love the story found in the Gospel of John in which Jesus utters that oft-quoted line: "Let any one of you who is without sin be the first to throw a stone at her" (John 8:7). Perhaps you will remember that, after the self-righteous circle of charlatans slowly slithered away, the woman was left standing there, probably utterly confused.

> Jesus straightened up and asked her, "Woman, where are they? Has no one condemned you?"
> "No one, sir," she said.
> "Then neither do I condemn you," Jesus declared. "Go now and leave your life of sin." (John 8:10-11)

Note that he did not say, "Don't worry about those old prudes; what you're doing is not so bad." No; he said, "Go and sin no more." He told her, "Don't live like that anymore."

It's not wrong to speak against immorality. The point of the story is that we never will change the world with stones in our hands and sins in our hearts.

May I say that again? We never will change the world with stones in our hands and sins in our hearts.

CONCLUSION

I STAND FIRMLY ON MY POSITION, yet I stand here humbly. Lots of bright and devoted Christians disagree with me. They pose questions of interpretation that are not easily dismissed. They ask difficult questions such as, "So, if a same-sex married couple decides they have been wrong, are they supposed to get a divorce?" and, "What about the ones Jesus referred to as 'eunuchs who were born that way' (Matthew 19:12)? Is that a potential reference to transgender people? Or to same-sex attracted people? If so, what does that have to say to the debate here?" These are questions for which there are no easy answers.

In Nigeria where we served as missionaries, I knew men with multiple wives who could not celebrate communion in their churches. When missionaries introduced the Christian faith, Christian ethics clashed with certain cultural realities. Polygamy represents a source of one of those clashes. Instead of asking polygamist men to divorce some of their wives, missionaries tried to find an appropriate way to oppose the practice and include the person. They came up with the idea that polygamist men could not take communion.

Now, I don't believe withholding communion is the right approach to Christian polygamists. However, I do understand how messy it can get when our understanding of Christian ethics is lived out in the "way things are." And I believe it will be messy for a season while we attempt to answer LGBT questions for which there are no easy answers.

Moreover, I understand that my position here could be hurtful to same-sex attracted people with whom I would love very much to have a positive relationship. I deeply regret that potential result and will do everything I can to build meaningful relationships—relationships through which I will certainly be enriched.

Yet my heart and head are settled on the position I have taken. I believe it is supported by Scripture as rightly interpreted.

My goal is the appropriate balance. We are going to have to find the balance that Jesus struck with the adulterous woman tossed at Jesus' feet by the stone-carrying religious leaders. He was kindhearted but not condoning. He was compassionately present with her without defending her choices. He did not dismiss the religious leaders' concern for morality, but neither did he tolerate their hypocritical condemnation. Somehow we are going to have to strike that very balance.

The way of compassionate morality is the way of Jesus and the way I believe we must take. The way of compassionate morality means extending our arms and hearts to people who are making bad sexual choices whether they are straight or gay, but not endorsing those choices. We should welcome imperfect people (like us), yet remember that the biblical bar is high for those who dare to offer spiritual leadership.

We obviously don't want to throw up our hands and say "anything goes." But we also don't want to fold our arms condescendingly like the Pharisees whom Jesus so often condemned. If we fold our arms, then people who are struggling with their sexual identity won't even give us the honor of a conversation. That includes our sons, daughters, grandsons, and granddaughters.

Believing that a sexual relationship between people of the same sex is wrong is one thing. Choosing to ignore, reject, bully, or loathe people who engage in those relationships is another.

A PROCESS AND A STATEMENT

If a church or denomination chooses to engage in some sort of process to address questions related to gay sexuality, expectations should be realistic. It is not likely, for example, that lots of people will change their minds about the rightness or wrongness of same-sex intimacy. Most people now seem to be deeply entrenched. However, some people will change their opinions on some matters. After a healthy process, people will be stretched, informed, and aware. Some will admit to seeing the topic in a new light and be able to articulate their positions more adeptly.

Most importantly, people can learn to see the opposition differently. While minds might not often change, hearts can. Relationships can be strengthened; assumptions can be corrected; labels can be dropped. I've seen that happen, and it is a beautiful thing.

Our church engaged in a six-month process (see appendix A) and issued a position statement (see appendix B). Of course that conversation was fraught with danger. We would not have embarked on such a treacherous journey without the deep conviction of our leaders that it was necessary.

Within our congregation I urged people to be willing to stretch as far in the direction of the opposing position as they could without violating their consciences. Of course, I did not ask anyone to disregard their sincere sense of the biblical message. I did, however, urge people to remember that there are equally sincere Christians who hold opposing views. I asked that people not contravene their convictions, but reminded everyone that if they could recognize and affirm the majority opinion of our church, that would be good for the fellowship and mission of our congregation.

There were those on each side of the debate who struggled with the Welcoming but Not Affirming approach that I advocate here (although we did not use those words in our written statement), and each had good arguments for their positions. Yet we emerged from our discussion with a powerful sense of unity.

Here are some things I need to communicate clearly: (1) our final decision was not unanimous, though the statement was approved by an overwhelming majority, (2) the process was painful for lots of people, and (3) I speak in this book only for myself and not for our congregation.

I also need to communicate that, despite the pain, tension, and complexities of our process, our people proved to be beautifully accommodating and collaborative for the sake of the precious fellowship and compelling mission of our church.

IT IS POSSIBLE

The late pastor Ed Dobson led his church in Grand Rapids to minister to gay people with HIV, though, as far as I know, he never wavered on what he considered to be the sinful nature of same-sex sexual practice. One person said to Dobson, "We understand where you stand, and know that you do not agree with us. But you still show the love of Jesus, and we're drawn to that."[1] Dobson and the church he led demonstrated that a church does not have to make a choice between morals and compassion.

High moral standards and Christian love are not mutually exclusive. I reject the idea that we cannot stand for biblical values and be caring at the same time. It is possible to love same-sex attracted people without being either condescending or condoning.

That will require people like me who hold a Traditional view to do more than sit around pontificating. It will require us to initiate loving relationships with people who are gay. It will require a softening of our tone without a relaxing of our convictions.

May God give us all the wisdom to find the balance between the crusader and the servant, and the Christ-like combination of morality and grace. To love God is to keep his commandments as best we can understand them. To love people is to extend grace. We cannot falter on either.

ACKNOWLEDGMENTS

This book began years ago and has expanded as I have done my best to guide multiple congregations through conversations around LGBT questions and in ministry in light of the present cultural debate. When I became pastor of the First Baptist Church of Huntsville, Alabama, in 2016, the congregation already had decided to have a church-wide discussion on the topic of same-sex relationships with the ultimate goal being some sort of statement. I then developed the booklet further, digging deeper into the topic and increasing the breadth of the booklet's content. When I did that, three women read the draft and helped improve my wording: Anne Stone, Diane Singer, and Sue McElyea. The ministerial staff of the First Baptist Church of Huntsville also read the draft and offered their invaluable insights.

Dr. Todd Still, dean of Baylor's Truett Seminary and a New Testament scholar, helped me make sure my Greek work was sound.

I'm grateful to Chris Backert and JR Rozko of Missio Alliance, who sent the manuscript to InterVarsity Press, and to Anna Gissing and other great folks at IVP who helped me shape this book.

My greatest debt is to the congregation of the First Baptist Church of Huntsville. They were courageously willing to wrestle with a difficult matter and did so with grace and civility. Much of what you will find in this book grew out of my experience with that wonderful church family.

APPENDIX A

A PROCESS

OUR CHURCH IS A RELATIVELY big tent church. We affirm women in ministry. We proclaim Jesus as the only means of salvation. We consider ourselves centrist Baptists.

Yet the church spoke overwhelmingly in favor of a Traditional position statement on LGBT topics. Losing people as a result was difficult, though not nearly as many people left as I thought might. There were also those who *came* to our church because they were looking for a church that was willing to address the topic, and they identified with the position we reached. While the losses were painful, the church actually emerged stronger at the end of the conversation.

Here is the process that our church followed in formulating and adopting a position statement. See appendix B for the position statement.

DISCOVERY

Week One: A Study Team was affirmed by the church.

Week Three: A suggested reading list of equal numbers of writers representing each viewpoint (see "For Further Reading" at the end of this book) was made available to the congregation.

Week Nine: My booklet (a predecessor to this book) on the topic was made available at the conclusion of worship services.

Week Twelve: A season of prayer and fasting began.

Weeks Fourteen, Fifteen, and Sixteen: I did a sermon series on Sunday mornings with question-and-answer sessions on Wednesday and Sunday evenings.

DISCUSSION

Weeks Fourteen, Fifteen, and Sixteen: We held church-wide conversations, including six listening sessions led by me, four listening sessions led by the Study Team, a direct email address to allow people to email the Study Team, and a secure, facilitated online opportunity for the posting of opinions.

DOCUMENT/DIRECTION

Weeks Sixteen through Nineteen: The Study Team met and worked on drafting a statement.

Weeks Twenty and Twenty-One: The Study Team presented a preliminary report to the Ministerial Staff for feedback and, one week later, to the Legal Committee.

Week Twenty-Two: The Study Team presented its report to the Leadership Council. At this point, the Leadership Council assumed responsibility for the document and prepared it for presentation to the deacons and ultimately to the congregation.

Week Twenty-Three: The Leadership Council presented the document to the deacons for affirmation.

DISCERNMENT

Week Twenty-Four: The proposed statement was distributed to the church.

DECISION

Week Twenty-Six: A vote to affirm the statement was held in a Sunday evening gathering.

The process is as important as the decision, and the process is particularly important for churches who reflect a broad diversity of opinions on this topic in particular. The process should . . .

be prayerfully deliberate,
offer plentiful opportunities for input and reflection,
ensure that those in the minority are not excluded, and
be led by skilled facilitators.

A process such as this should be entered with the full knowledge that it will be difficult, emotional, and potentially divisive. The best that most churches can hope for is substantial agreement.

By the way, it is important to remember that a statement by one congregation does not implicate, accuse, or question the orthodoxy of congregations who have a different position. A good statement also does not label or marginalize those holding a minority viewpoint. A statement is simply declaring, "This is what a majority of our church members believe to be true."

APPENDIX B

A STATEMENT ON SEXUALITY
FIRST BAPTIST CHURCH, HUNTSVILLE
(APPROVED NOVEMBER 13, 2016)

ROOTED IN THE MESSAGE of Scripture as we understand it, and consistent with Christian teaching through 2,000 years, we, the members of First Baptist Church of Huntsville, reaffirm the following beliefs regarding sexuality:

- We believe sexuality is a beautiful gift established by a loving God who knows a gift of such great value can reach its potential only within the covenant of marriage.

Genesis 2:18, 22-24; Proverbs 5:18-19; Matthew 19:4-6; 1 Corinthians 7:3-5

- We believe marriage is a divine institution between a man and a woman.

Genesis 2:18, 22-24; Mark 10:6-9

- We believe any act of sexual intimacy outside of marriage is incompatible with biblical teaching.

Exodus 20:14; Romans 1:26-27; 1 Corinthians 6:18-20; 1 Corinthians 7:2; 1 Thessalonians 4:3-4; Hebrews 13:4

- We believe all of us belonging to a church family requires a commitment to increasing holiness in every area of our lives through the power of the Holy Spirit, the practice of spiritual disciplines, and the support of our brothers and sisters in Christ.

Romans 12:1-2; Philippians 2:1-5; Titus 3:5; Hebrews 10:24-25; 1 Peter 1:13-16; 1 John 3:1-3

- We believe spiritual leadership carries a high standard of behavior. That behavior includes, but is not limited to, sexual choices.

Matthew 18:6; 1 Timothy 3:1-12; 1 Timothy 4:12; James 3:1; 1 Peter 5:3

- We believe all persons are created in the image of God and are deserving of respect and compassion regardless of their sexual orientation or choices.

Genesis 1:27; Genesis 5:1-2; Mark 12:28-31; Colossians 3:12-14; 2 Thessalonians 1:3

- We believe the diversity of our congregation on complex issues enriches our journey and our ministry.

John 17:22-23; Romans 15:5-6; Ephesians 4:1-5; 2 Corinthians 13:11; Philippians 1:9-11; Philippians 2:1-5

- We believe none of us is without a desperate need for God's grace.

Luke 5:31-32; John 1:16; John 8:1-11; Romans 3:23-24; Ephesians 2:8-9

This position statement is our best attempt at balancing grace and truth, the two equally important facets of the Christian faith embodied in the Lord Jesus.

IMPLICATIONS FOR MEMBERSHIP AND LEADERSHIP

Membership

As members of FBC, we uphold the biblical standard of holiness, which would include such practices as truthfulness in business dealings, honesty in our academic pursuits, sincerity in our relationships, and fairness in our dealings with people who might otherwise be treated unfairly. We also teach the biblical standard of sexual purity while emphasizing that the important decision is to be sexually pure from this point forward. Membership in

First Baptist Church implies a public commitment to faith in Jesus and a willingness to undergo, with others on the same journey, ongoing transformation. Church membership requires from present and potential members a commitment to ethical and moral purity. We welcome among us those who are willing to strive alongside us toward ever-increasing holiness and spiritual maturity.

Leadership

We believe spiritual leadership carries a high standard of behavior. That behavior includes, though it is not limited to, sexual choices. Therefore, a sexual life that is above reproach is requisite for ordination to the role of deacon or to vocational ministry. We further expect a life of sexual purity for those teaching in the discipleship programs of the church, such as in Sunday school and small groups, and those serving on the Leadership Council.

DISCUSSION GUIDE

PART ONE

1. What are your personal biases in approaching this topic? What prejudices, even discomfort, will you have to set aside in order to consider this topic honestly? If you are discussing this book in a group of people in which there is a high level of trust, have each person answer these questions openly. And be careful not to condemn people for being honest about their preconceptions.

2. What have you assumed about the "cause(s)" of same-sex attraction? Why do you believe you have made those assumptions? Could your assumptions be wrong?

3. Are there varying opinions on the topic of same-sex relationships within your congregation? Or would you say there is widespread agreement on the topic? No matter your answer, what would you say are the strengths and weaknesses of your congregation when it comes to discussing this topic?

4. Go to Philippians 4 and read the story of Euodia and Syntyche. What can you learn from their dispute, and Paul's counsel to them, about your disagreements with fellow Christians?

5. Do you know someone who has an opinion about this topic that is very different from yours? Would you be

willing to ask that person to articulate their reasoning behind their position, without defending your own? In other words, would you be willing to listen purely for the sake of learning, and not offer your opinion?

6. In this section you read: "So, let's take 'judge not' seriously, but let's not take it further than it was intended. The Bible gives us a balance." How do you understand the phrase "judge not" as it applies to Christians and morals? Based on what you read here, how would you describe the Bible's balance when it comes to "judging"?

7. What are some of the unfair labels that you have heard given to people in this debate over the topic of same-sex relationships?

PART TWO

1. Take a few minutes to articulate the arguments given by those whose position is different from your own. If you are a Traditionalist, describe the Affirming position. If you are on the Affirming side, describe the Traditional position. Try to put yourself in the position of one on the other side of the debate, and do so honestly and as thoroughly as you can.

2. Bishop Spong refers to Paul's "ill-informed, culturally biased prejudices." What is your opinion on the position that our experience and reasoning today are simply different from the witness of the Bible, and thus more reliable in the twenty-first century context?

3. William Webb contends that, while the New Testament never speaks with the clarity we would like about slavery and the role and value of women, there is a clear progression within the New Testament toward the condemnation of slavery and the affirmation of women. When

it comes to sexual behavior between members of the same sex, however, the New Testament reflects and even reinforces the same restrictive tone we find in the Old Testament. What do you think of Webb's "redemptive-movement hermeneutic"?

4. Some contend that having a close friend or family member who is gay gives one the ability to speak with unique authority on the topic. Others contend that having a close friend or family member who is gay minimizes one's objectivity in speaking to the topic. What do you think?

5. What is your view of divorce? How is divorce different from same-sex intimacy? How does your view of divorce inform your position on same-sex relationships?

6. Do you believe, as Robert Gagnon posited, that if the Corinthian Christians had written to Paul and explained that in their church were two men in an intimate relationship who were truly in love, that Paul would have responded, "Oh, I'm not talking about them"?

PART THREE

1. Do you agree that, in our society, sexuality has been viewed as more central to our identity than is healthy? Explain your answer.

2. How do you view the call to abstinence for those who are attracted to persons of the same sex?

3. In this section we noted two conflicting perspectives. One is, "If we don't take a stance young people will be encouraged to experiment with same-sex relationships." The other perspective is, "If we do take a strong stance they will not ask for help and will dangerously internalize their struggles."

   Do these perspectives resonate with you?

4. Put yourself in the position of a same-sex attracted Christian. Would you feel welcomed in a church that had affirmed a position that says, in essence, "We welcome everyone to our worship, fellowship, and membership, but we will not invite people who are in active same-sex relationships into leadership"?

5. What are the pros and cons of a church or denomination taking a position on this topic?

6. As you pray, "Search me, God," (Psalm 139:23), are there things in your own life that you need to confess and ask God to clean up?

7. Name one positive step (not mentioned in this book) that would help the Christian family deal in a healthy way with this explosive topic of sexuality.

NOTES

"WELCOMING?" (AN INTRODUCTION)

[1]Eddie Kirkland, "Here and Now," *Songs at North Point*, Eddie Kirkland Music, 2011.

CHAPTER 1: MEANINGS, MOTIVES, REGRETS, AND HOPES

[1]Justin Lee, *Torn: Rescuing the Gospel from the Gays-vs.-Christians Debate* (New York: Jericho Books, 2012), 49-50.

[2]Rosaria Champagne Butterfield, *Openness Unhindered: Further Thoughts of an Unlikely Convert on Sexual Identity and Union with Christ* (Pittsburgh, PA: Crown & Covenant Publications, 2015), Kindle edition, location 243-44.

CHAPTER 2: A DIFFICULT, KNOTTY, POTENTIALLY THORNY CONVERSATION

[1]Frederick William Faber (1814-1863), "There's a Wideness in God's Mercy."

[2]Some content from Travis Collins, "A Krispy Kreme for the Road," sermon delivered at Bon Air Baptist Church, Richmond, Virginia, February 26, 2014.

[3]Ken Wilson, *A Letter to My Congregation* (Ann Arbor, MI: Front Edge Publishing, 2014), 104.

[4]John Shore, *Unfair: Christians and the LGBT Question* (North Charleston, SC: CreateSpace Independent Publishing Platform, 2013), 171-72.

[5]Stanley J. Grenz, *Welcoming but Not Affirming* (Louisville, KY: Westminster John Knox, 1998), 9.

[6]Wilson, *A Letter To My Congregation*, 35.

[7]Debra Hirsch, *Redeeming Sex* (Downers Grove, IL: InterVarsity Press, 2015), 162.

CHAPTER 3: THE TERRIFYING BEAUTY
OF A DIVERSE CHURCH OR DENOMINATION

[1]Dr. Seuss with Jack Prelutsky and Lane Smith, *Hooray for Diffendoofer Day!* (New York: Knopf Doubleday, 1998), 22.

[2]John Ortberg, *All the Places to Go . . . How Will You Know?* (Carol Stream, IL: Tyndale House Publishers, 2015), 30.

[3]John G. Stackhouse Jr., "How to Produce an Egalitarian Man," in Alan F. Johnson, ed., *How I Changed My Mind About Women in Leadership* (Grand Rapids: Zondervan, 2010), 237.

[4]Ibid.

[5]Tony Cartledge, "N.C. Pastor Resigns After Conflict over National Politics," *Baptist News Global*, May 24, 2005, https://baptistnews.com/article /ncpastorresignsafterconflictovernationalpolitics/#.WKY_VfkrKyI.

CHAPTER 4: THE AFFIRMING POSITION

[1]David P. Gushee, *Changing Our Mind* (Canton, MI: Read the Spirit Books, 2015), 144.

[2]Matthew Vines, *God and the Gay Christian* (New York: Penguin Random House, 2014), 156, 162.

[3]Ibid., 2.

[4]Colby Martin, *UnClobber: Rethinking our Misuse of the Bible on Homosexuality* (Louisville, KY: Westminster John Knox, 2016), 164-65. See also Ken Wilson, *A Letter to My Congregation* (Ann Arbor, MI: Front Edge Publishing, 2014), 60.

[5]John Shore, *Unfair: Christians and the LGBT Question* (North Charleston, SC: CreateSpace Independent Publishing Platform, 2013), 171-72.

[6]James V. Brownson, *Bible, Gender, Sexuality: Reframing the Church's Debate on Same-Sex Relationships* (Grand Rapids: Eerdmans, 2013), 168-69.

[7]William Loader, "Homosexuality and the Bible," in Preston Sprinkle, ed., *Two Views on Homosexuality, the Bible, and the Church* (Grand Rapids: Zondervan, 2016), 20.

[8]Ibid., 45.

[9]Ibid., 68. See also Luke Timothy Johnson, "Homosexuality and the Church," *Commonweal*, June 11, 2007, www.commonwealmagazine.org/homo sexuality-church-1.

[10]Walter Wink, "Biblical Perspectives on Homosexuality," *The Christian Century*, November 7, 1979, no. 46A.

[11]John Shelby Spong, *Living in Sin? A Bishop Rethinks Human Sexuality* (San Francisco: HarperCollins, 1988), 151.

[12]Ibid., 152.

[13]Gushee, *Changing Our Mind*, 5.

[14]See also Johnson, "Homosexuality and the Church."

[15]Wilson, *A Letter To My Congregation*, 35.

[16]Gregory A. Boyd, *The Myth of a Christian Nation* (Grand Rapids: Zondervan, 2007), 137.

[17]Shore, *Unfair*, 4.

[18]Mark Achtemeier, *The Bible's Yes to Same-Sex Marriage* (Louisville, KY: Westminster John Knox, 2014), 69-70. See also Luke Timothy Johnson, *Scripture & Discernment* (Nashville: Abingdon Press, 1996), and Martin, *UnClobber*, 29, 104-6.

[19]Spong, *Living in Sin?*, 23, 80.

CHAPTER 5: THE TRADITIONAL POSITION

[1]See Richard B. Hays, *The Moral Vision of the New Testament* (San Francisco: HarperCollins, 1996), 388-89, 394.

[2]See Robert A. J. Gagnon, *The Bible and Homosexual Practice* (Nashville: Abingdon Press, 2001), 347-351, and William J. Webb, *Slaves, Women & Homosexuals* (Downers Grove, IL: InterVarsity Press, 2001), 156.

[3]See Matthew Vines, *God and the Gay Christian* (New York: Penguin Random House, 2014), 32.

[4]Kevin DeYoung, *What Does the Bible Really Teach about Homosexuality?* (Wheaton, IL: Crossway, 2015), 83ff.

[5]Steve Yamaguchi, "N. T. Wright on Debate about Homosexuality 4," YouTube, March 11, 2009, www.youtube.com/watch?v=YpQHGPGejKs.

[6]Brent Pickett, "Homosexuality," *Stanford Encyclopedia of Philosophy*, July 5, 2015, http://plato.stanford.edu/entries/homosexuality; See also Plato, *Symposium*, 360 BCE, translated by Benjamin Jowett, http://classics.mit.edu/Plato/symposium.html.

[7]Stanley J. Grenz, *Welcoming but Not Affirming* (Louisville, KY: Westminster John Knox, 1998), 137.

[8]Gagnon, *The Bible and Homosexual Practice*, 328-29.

[9]James D. G. Dunn, *Romans 1-8*, Word Biblical Commentary (Waco, TX: Word Books, 1988).

[10]See DeYoung, *What Does the Bible Really Teach About Homosexuality?*, 54; See also Dale Moody, "Romans," *The Broadman Bible Commentary*, Clifton Allen, ed. (Nashville: Broadman, 1970), 171.

[11]See Charles H. Talbert, *Romans*, Smyth & Helwys Bible Commentary (Macon, GA: Smyth & Helwys, 2002), 66-67; See also Dunn, *Romans 1-8*, 66.

[12]John Stott, *Same-Sex Partnerships?* (Grand Rapids: Fleming H. Revell, 1998), 43.

[13]See also Luke Timothy Johnson, "Homosexuality and the Church," *Commonweal*, June 11, 2007, www.commonwealmagazine.org/homosexuality-church-1.

[14]Vines, *God and the Gay Christian*, 21.

[15]John Shore, *Unfair: Christians and the LGBT Question* (North Charleston, SC: CreateSpace Independent Publishing Platform, 2013), 182-83.

[16]Hays, *The Moral Vision of the New Testament*, 380.

[17]Mark Achtemeier, *The Bible's Yes to Same-Sex Marriage* (Louisville, KY: Westminster John Knox, 2014), 73.

[18]Ibid., 24-25.

[19]Wilson, *A Letter to My Congregation* (Ann Arbor, MI: Front Edge Publishing, 2014), 50.

[20]Gagnon, *The Bible and Homosexual Practice*, 442.

[21]See, for example, Karen Grigsby Bates, "African-Americans Question Comparing Gay Rights Movement to Civil Rights," NPR, WBEZ Chicago, July 2, 2015, www.npr.org/2015/07/02/419554758/african-americans-question-comparing-gay-rights-movement-to-civil-rights; See also Eve Conant, "Are Gay Rights 'Civil Rights'?", *Newsweek*, www.newsweek.com/are-gay-rights-civil-rights-69121.

[22]See Gagnon, *The Bible and Homosexual Practice*, 187-88, 192, 227-28, 437; and also DeYoung, *What Does the Bible Really Teach About Homosexuality?*, 227-28.

[23]Walter Wink, "Biblical Perspectives on Homosexuality," *The Christian Century*, November 7, 1979, no. 46A.

[24]Stott, *Same-Sex Partnerships?*, 54.

CHAPTER 6: WHAT DOES THE BIBLE SAY?

[1]See James D. G. Dunn, *Romans 1-8*, Word Biblical Commentary (Waco, TX: Word Books, 1988), 65; see also Charles H. Talbert, *Romans*, Smyth & Helwys Bible Commentary (Macon, GA: Smyth & Helwys, 2002), 65-67.

[2]Richard B. Hays, *The Moral Vision of the New Testament* (San Francisco: HarperCollins, 1996), 386.

[3]Paul J. Achthemeier, *Romans, Interpretation: A Bible Commentary for Teaching and Preaching* (Louisville, KY: Westminster John Knox, 1985), 41-42.

[4]See, for example, Mark Achtemeier, *The Bible's Yes to Same-Sex Marriage* (Louisville, KY: Westminster John Knox, 2014), 98-100; see also Brownson, *Bible, Gender, Sexuality* (Grand Rapids: Eerdmans, 2013), 82-83.

[5]See, for example, William Loader, "Homosexuality in the Bible," in Preston Sprinkle, ed., *Two Views on Homosexuality, the Bible, and the Church* (Grand Rapids: Zondervan, 2016), 34, 103.

[6]A. T. Hanson in William D. Mounce, *Pastoral Epistles*, Word Biblical Commentary (Nashville: Thomas Nelson Publishers, 2000), 39.

[7]John R. W. Stott, *The Message of 1 Timothy and Titus*, The Bible Speaks Today (Downers Grove, IL: InterVarsity Press, 1996), 49.

[8]Gordon D. Fee, *1 & 2 Timothy, Titus*, Understanding the Bible Commentary Series (Grand Rapids: Baker Books, 1988), 46.

[9]William J. Webb, *Slaves, Women & Homosexuals* (Downers Grove, IL: InterVarsity Press, 2001), 16.

[10]Ibid., 60-61.

[11]Ibid., 87-88.

[12]Ibid., 82; see also Hays, *The Moral Vision of the New Testament*, 389.

[13]Webb, *Slaves, Women & Homosexuals*, 39.

CHAPTER 7: WHAT SHOULD A SAME-SEX ATTRACTED CHRISTIAN DO?

[1]Mark Yarhouse, *Homosexuality and the Christian* (Bloomington, MN: Bethany House Publishers, 2010), 41.

[2]Ibid., 40-43.

[3]Stanley J. Grenz, *Welcoming but Not Affirming* (Louisville, KY: Westminster John Knox, 1998), 126.

[4]Ibid.

[5]Richard B. Hays, *The Moral Vision of the New Testament* (San Francisco: HarperCollins, 1996), 402.

[6]James V. Brownson, *Bible, Gender, Sexuality: Reframing the Church's Debate on Same-Sex Relationships* (Grand Rapids: Eerdmans, 2013), 177; see also Mark Achtemeier, *The Bible's Yes to Same-Sex Marriage* (Louisville, KY: Westminster John Knox, 2014), 10-13.

[7]John Shore, *Unfair: Christians and the LGBT Question* (North Charleston, SC: CreateSpace Independent Publishing Platform, 2013), 132.

[8]Wesley Hill, *Washed and Waiting: Reflections on Christian Faithfulness & Homosexuality* (Grand Rapids: Zondervan, 2016), 171.

[9]Ibid., 95.

[10]Debra Hirsch, *Redeeming Sex: Naked Conversations About Sexuality and Spirituality* (Downers Grove, IL: InterVarsity Press, 2015), 58-59; see also 125-29.

[11]Stephen R. Holmes, "Christ, Scripture, and Spiritual Friendship," in Preston Sprinkle, ed., *Two Views on Homosexuality, the Bible, and the Church* (Grand Rapids: Zondervan, 2016), 183.

[12]See Yarhouse, *Homosexuality and the Christian*, 166, 175.

[13]Ed Shaw, *Same-Sex Attraction and the Church* (Downers Grove, IL: InterVarsity Press, 2015), 22.

[14]Ibid., 115.

[15]Kevin DeYoung, *What Does the Bible Really Teach About Homosexuality?* (Wheaton, IL: Crossway, 2015), 119.

[16]Philip Yancey, *What's So Amazing About Grace?* (Grand Rapids: Zondervan, 1997), 166.

CHAPTER 8: WE CAN'T JUST SING KUMBAYA FOREVER

[1]David P. Gushee, *Changing Our Mind* (Canton, MI: Read the Spirit Books, 2015), 21, 43.

[2]Debra Hirsch, *Redeeming Sex: Naked Conversations About Sexuality and Spirituality* (Downers Grove, IL: InterVarsity Press, 2015), 197.

CHAPTER 9: WELCOMING BUT NOT AFFIRMING AND MUTUALLY TRANSFORMING

[1]Philip Yancey, *What's So Amazing About Grace?* (Grand Rapids: Zondervan, 1997), 70.

[2]Joseph R. Cooke, *Celebration of Grace* (Grand Rapids: Zondervan, 1991), 13.

[3]Stanley J. Grenz, *Welcoming but Not Affirming* (Louisville, KY: Westminster John Knox, 1998), 1-2.

[4]Richard B. Hays, *The Moral Vision of the New Testament* (San Francisco: HarperCollins, 1996), 401.

[5]Justin Lee, *Torn: Rescuing the Gospel from the Gays-vs.-Christians Debate* (New York: Jericho Books, 2012), 247.

[6]Hays, *The Moral Vision of the New Testament,* 400-401.

[7]David Fitch, "'The Welcoming and Mutually Transforming Community Among the LGBTQ: An Example and Some Questions," Missio Alliance, August 30, 2010, www.missioalliance.org/the-welcoming-and-mutually -transforming-community-among-the-lgbtq-an-example-and-some -questions/.

[8]Tony Campolo, "For the Record," June 8, 2015, http://tonycampolo.org /for-the-record-tony-campolo-releases-a-new-statement/#.Vw8QfjArLNP.

CHAPTER 10: WHAT CAN WE DO?

[1]Material first published by Travis Collins, "4 Confessions from the Church to the LGBT Community," Seedbed, July 25, 2016, https://www.seedbed .com/4-confessions-church-lgbtq-community-travis-collins/.

[2]Andrew Marin, *Us Versus Us* (Colorado Springs, CO: NavPress, 2016), xix.

[3]Ibid., 65.

[4]David P. Gushee, *Changing Our Mind* (Canton, MI: Read the Spirit Books, 2015), 136 ff.

[5]Marin, *Us Versus Us,* xiii.

[6]Richard B. Hays, *The Moral Vision of the New Testament* (San Francisco: HarperCollins, 1996), 381.

[7]Mark A. Yarhouse, *Homosexuality and the Christian* (Bloomington, MN: Bethany House Publishers, 2010), 48-50.

[8]Ibid., 48-51.

[9]Ralph E. Longshore in K. Owen White, *Messages on Stewardship* (Grand Rapids: Baker Books, 1963), 140-141.

[10]Dorothy Day, *The Long Loneliness* (New York: HarperOne, 2009) 18-19, 35.

CONCLUSION

[1]Quoted in Philip Yancey, *What's So Amazing About Grace?* (Grand Rapids: Zondervan, 1997), 169.

FOR FURTHER READING

AFFIRMING VIEW

Achtemeier, Mark. *The Bible's Yes to Same-Sex Marriage: An Evangelical's Change of Heart*. Louisville, KY: Westminster John Knox, 2014.

Brownson, James V. *Bible, Gender, Sexuality: Reframing the Church's Debate on Same-Sex Relationships*. Grand Rapids: Eerdmans, 2013.

Gushee, David P. *Changing Our Mind*. Canton, MI: Read the Spirit Books, 2015.

Lee, Justin. *Torn: Rescuing the Gospel from the Gays-vs.-Christians Debate*. New York: Jericho Books, 2012.

Martin, Colby. *UnClobber: Rethinking our Misuse of the Bible on Homosexuality*. Louisville, KY: Westminster John Knox, 2016.

Shore, John. *Unfair: Christians and the LGBT Question*. North Charleston, SC: CreateSpace Independent Publishing, 2013.

Spong, John Shelby. *Living in Sin? A Bishop Rethinks Human Sexuality*. San Francisco: HarperCollins, 1988.

Vines, Matthew. *God and the Gay Christian: The Biblical Case in Support of Same-Sex Relationships*. New York: Penguin Random House, 2014.

Wilson, Ken. *A Letter to my Congregation: An Evangelical Pastor's Path to Embracing People Who Are Gay, Lesbian, Bisexual, and Transgender into the Company of Jesus*. Ann Arbor, MI: Front Edge Publishing, 2014.

TRADITIONAL VIEW

Butterfield, Rosaria Champagne. *Openness Unhindered: Further Thoughts of an Unlikely Convert on Sexual Identity and Union with Christ*. Pittsburgh, PA: Crown & Covenant Publications, 2015.

DeYoung, Kevin. *What Does the Bible Really Teach About Homosexuality?* Wheaton, IL: Crossway, 2015.

Gagnon, Robert A. *The Bible and Homosexual Practice: Texts and Hermeneutics.* Nashville: Abingdon Press, 2001.

Grenz, Stanley J. *Welcoming but Not Affirming: An Evangelical Response to Homosexuality.* Louisville, KY: Westminster John Knox, 1998.

Hays, Richard B. *The Moral Vision of the New Testament: A Contemporary Introduction to New Testament Ethics.* San Francisco: HarperCollins, 1996.

McDowell, Sean and Stonestreet, John. *Same-Sex Marriage: A Thoughtful Approach to God's Design for Marriage.* Grand Rapids: Baker Books, 2014.

Stott, John. *Same-Sex Partnerships? A Christian Perspective.* Grand Rapids: Fleming H. Revell, 1998.

Webb, William J. *Slaves, Women & Homosexuals: Exploring the Hermeneutics of Cultural Analysis.* Downers Grove, IL: InterVarsity Press, 2001.

Yarhouse, Mark A. *Homosexuality and the Christian: A Guide for Parents, Pastors, and Friends.* Bloomington, MN: Bethany House Publishers, 2010.

COMPETING VIEWS

Sprinkle, Preston, ed. *Two Views on Homosexuality, the Bible and the Church.* Grand Rapids: Zondervan, 2016.

SAME-SEX ATTRACTED PEOPLE
WHO CHOOSE CHASTITY

Coles, Gregory. *Single, Gay, Christian: A Personal Journey of Faith and Sexual Identity.* Downers Grove, IL: InterVarsity Press, 2017.

Hill, Wesley. *Washed and Waiting: Reflections on Christian Faithfulness and Homosexuality.* Grand Rapids: Zondervan, 2010.

Shaw, Ed. *Same-Sex Attraction and the Church: The Surprising Plausibility of the Celibate Life.* Downers Grove, IL: InterVarsity Press, 2015.

THE BIBLE AND SEXUALITY

Hirsch, Debra. *Redeeming Sex: Naked Conversations About Sexuality and Spirituality.* Downers Grove, IL: InterVarsity Press, 2015.

FAITH AND THE SAME-SEX ATTRACTED COMMUNITY

Marin, Andrew. *Us versus Us: The Untold Story of Religion and the LGBT Community.* Colorado Spring, CO: NavPress, 2016.

Missio Alliance

Missio Alliance has arisen in response to the shared voice of pastors and ministry leaders from across the landscape of North American Christianity for a new "space" of togetherness and reflection amid the issues and challenges facing the church in our day. We are united by a desire for a fresh expression of evangelical faith, one significantly informed by the global evangelical family. Lausanne's Cape Town Commitment, "A Confession of Faith and a Call to Action," provides an excellent guidepost for our ethos and aims.

Through partnerships with schools, denominational bodies, ministry organizations, and networks of churches and leaders, Missio Alliance addresses the most vital theological and cultural issues facing the North American Church in God's mission today. We do this primarily by convening gatherings, curating resources, and catalyzing innovation in leadership formation.

Rooted in the core convictions of evangelical orthodoxy, the ministry of Missio Alliance is animated by a strong and distinctive theological identity that emphasizes

Comprehensive Mutuality: Advancing the partnered voice and leadership of women and men among the beautiful diversity of the body of Christ across the lines of race, culture, and theological heritage.

Hopeful Witness: Advancing a way of being the people of God in the world that reflects an unwavering and joyful hope in the lordship of Christ in the church and over all things.

Church in Mission: Advancing a vision of the local church in which our identity and the power of our testimony is found and expressed through our active participation in God's mission in the world.

In partnership with InterVarsity Press, we are pleased to offer a line of resources authored by a diverse range of theological practitioners. The resources in this series are selected based on the important way in which they address and embody these values, and thus, the unique contribution they offer in equipping Christian leaders for fuller and more faithful participation in God's mission.

missioalliance.org | twitter.com/missioalliance | facebook.com/missioalliance

More Titles from
InterVarsity Press and Missio Alliance

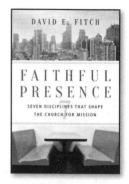

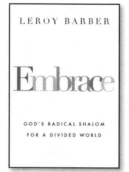

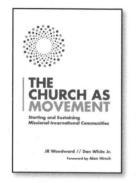

The Church as Movement
978-0-8308-4133-2

Embrace
978-0-8308-4471-5

Faithful Presence
978-0-8308-4127-1

Paradoxology
978-0-8308-4504-0

Redeeming Sex
978-0-8308-3639-0

White Awake
978-0-8308-4393-0